Other Books
By
Richard Harvey

Cutting Edge Blackjack (0-9672182-7-6, $19.95)
The Santa Fe Reporter wrote: "Harvey's newest book is the result of three years of computer studies that completely disprove the effectiveness of methods used since the late 50's." Midwest Gaming & Travel hailed *Cutting Edge Blackjack* for its bold new approach to game strategy, saying its methods will make players much more successful. It includes *the first-ever method for identifying the facedown cards at 1- & 2-deck tables. Packed* with illustrations and charts, this sets a new standard, giving players greater precision in making card moves and bets than ever before. This *has no peer.*

Blackjack The SMART Way (0-9672182-5-X, $19.95)
This bestseller was named one of the 1000 best books by Top 1000 Amazon.com reviewer James Anderson III: "This blackjack strategy book gives good advice to players of all skill levels. If you play blackjack even occasionally, you owe it to yourself to get this book and increase your winning percentage. *Highly* recommended!" The Colorado Gambler says it "will turn any player into a winner." The Weekly Alibi says: "It makes sense. It makes money. It works. That's the bottom line." Akin to Part 1 to *Cutting Edge Blackjack's* Part 2, its methods achieved an amazing *88% winning rate* in pre-publication tests!

Richard Harvey's Blackjack PowerPrep Session (0-9672182-6-8, $14.95)
Written by the man called "a blackjack guru" by Rick Alm of the Kansas City Star and "the Blackjack King!" by KKFN's Irv Brown, this Compact Disc audio book gives *Blackjack The SMART Way* readers their essential pre-casino practice session. Pop it in your car's CD player as you head to the casino!

For more information and Richard Harvey's free monthly blackjack tips please visit www.blackjacktoday.com.

Also From Mystic Ridge Books
www.mysticridgebooks.com

20 Women Reveal
The Most Intimate
Details Of Their
Best Lovemaking
Experiences

www.baringit.com

Baring It All
Edited by
Layla Shilkret
Read it with
your lover and
watch what
happens!

Mystic Ridge Books: Great Reads for a Diverse Set
of Interests & Pleasures -- For Adults & Children ·

Our growing line of fine books covers everything from Love
& Intimacy to Children's Fiction. Mail the form below to
Mystic Ridge Books, P.O. Box 66930, Albuquerque, NM
87193 for our complete catalog.

Name:_____

Address:_____

_____

Email:_____

Kinds of books you like:_____

_____

NEW Ways to Win MORE at Blackjack

by Richard Harvey

THE BEST OF THE BLACKJACK INNOVATOR'S SYNDICATED BLACKJACK COLUMNS

(VOL. 1)

Dedicated to the memory of my cousin Marilyn

MYSTIC RIDGE BOOKS

ALBUQUERQUE, NEW MEXICO

Published by:
MYSTIC RIDGE BOOKS
P.O. BOX 66930
ALBUQUERQUE, NM 87193-6930

Find us on the World Wide Web at:
http://www.mysticridgebooks.com
http://www.blackjacktoday.com
Email: mysticridge@comcast.net
MYSTIC RIDGE BOOKS is a division of Mystic Ridge Productions, Inc.

Legal Disclaimer:
The purpose of this book is to prepare you to deal well with the blackjack environment, and to make you a smart, *conservative*, winning player, over time. NO book should guarantee winnings every time you play, because of many variables. These include your personality and your ability to concentrate, study, memorize and learn the author's methods and concepts; your level of discipline and conscientiousness in following the author's instructions; and the differing rules and restrictions of the different casinos at which you choose to play. There are rarely huge jackpots to be won in any one sitting, and blackjack is unlikely to make you a millionaire. You must never go to the casino hoping for and expecting huge, Lottery-sized riches, nor should you bet or play beyond your financial limitations. ONLY play if you can keep it in the realm of a fun activity and NOT an obsession. Those who are inclined to ignore the author's advice and become addicted to gambling, please DON'T PLAY BLACKJACK; contact Gambler's Anonymous or a similar help group.

PRINTED AND BOUND IN THE UNITED STATES OF AMERICA.

———
Library of Congress Cataloging-in-Publication Data

Harvey, Richard, 1960-
    New ways to win more at blackjack : the best of the
blackjack innovator's syndicated blackjack columns / by
Richard Harvey.— 1st ed.
        p. cm.
    Includes bibliographical references and index.
    ISBN 0-9672182-9-2 (alk. paper)
    1. Blackjack (Game) 2. Gambling systems. I. Title.
    GV1295.B55H397 2004
    796.4'23—dc22

                                          2004007672

Table of Contents

Author's Note

It was with great pleasure that I worked on this book. Although my syndicated columns are read by many, they are still unavailable in some parts of the United States and the world at large, and that's a shame. (For a way you can help bring my weekly columns to your favorite newspaper or magazine, see the "P.S." on the following page.)

The chapters in this book represent more than 52 of my columns. I rewrote and added material to most of them, and some are condensations of multi-part columns, so this book represents more than a year's worth of advice.

I was pleased that Mystic Ridge Books decided to release this book. I made a lot of breakthroughs in my card-based computer studies into card behavior, shuffling and the game of blackjack that could not be fit into *Blackjack The SMART Way* and *Cutting Edge Blackjack, some of which you'll find in these columns*. There's fresh material in *New Ways to Win MORE at Blackjack* that you cannot find anywhere else. Plus, here, I have been able to simplify some of my more complex concepts and methods so players of all levels can profit from them. (Because this is a book of columns, some important concepts are discussed more than once. But, I think you'll agree, these ideas *need* reinforcing.)

Now don't forget to visit **www.blackjacktoday.com** each month, for my free online advice column. It will also alert you to seminar dates and new book releases -- such as the imminent release of my new audio book, *Richard Harvey's Blackjack PowerPrep Session.* A companion to *Blackjack The SMART Way*, it covers one often-neglected aspect of my system: the practicing and prepping you absolutely need to do in advance of every trip to the casino. If you don't know how to go about doing this, this does the work for you.

I owe all of you a debt of gratitude for being such avid fans and readers. It makes me glad that so many of you have told me -- in letters, emails, phone calls to talk shows on which I've appeared, and in face-to-face conversations at seminars and book events -- that my methods have made you successful beyond your wildest dreams. That makes it all worthwhile. So, to you, my heartfelt thanks.

See you at one of my book events, seminars, or at the table. Until then...

Best Wishes,

Richard Harvey

P.S. You can do your part to bring my weekly syndicated column to your local newpaper or magazine. Call them and ask to speak to the publisher. Tell them you'd like them to carry my column. They might not realize it's available. If they're interested, please ask them to call Mystic Ridge Books to set things in motion. My publisher's number is 1-877-977-2121. It's that easy!

Is The Strategy You're Using Faulty?

Many of the concepts in my books are radically new, and, by and large, have been welcomed by players, most of which are eager to get the latest information on getting a greater edge on the house.

From time to time, however, a Doubting Thomas has emailed me, clinging to the ways of the past, in an attempt to disprove my criticisms of the blackjack methods that have largely been in place since 1961.

So, in *Cutting Edge Blackjack*, I detailed a dozen or so ways in which the early blackjack computer researchers went wrong – in their pre-research assumptions, their conducting of research, and then the conclusions they reached after the data was in.

Here, I want to discuss one of these flaws – their attempt to simplify the game by distilling the results of millions of rounds of computer-simulated blackjack rounds, and suggesting a Basic Strategy that was based upon the average outcomes of all of those rounds.

2

New Ways To Win MORE At Blackjack

First of all, understand that you are betting, in any given round, on what the results will be in that round only; not on what the numbers would be if eight million, or 150 million rounds were going to be played. There's a big difference.

But, let's look at this situation from a different angle. Here's how an Old School blackjack researcher, for instance, would have devised strategy for the game of baseball:

First, he would have used his computer to *simulate* the game. How would that work? He'd use its random number generator to simulate how each player fared at the plate. Then, he'd tally millions and millions of batters' pretend results to come up with a simplified approach to pitching, outfield placement, etc.

He'd have numbers indicating how each pitch *location* and *type* of pitch performed, in terms of producing batter outs. In other words, he'd take the collective results of the simulations he'd done (all players, all teams) and conclude that pitchers should deliver just one particular pitch to just one particular location for each batter, no matter what team, no matter what the strengths or weakness of each batter were, because that one specific type of pitch statistically performed the best, over millions and millions of computer-simulated batting experiences.

Ridiculous, right?

And here's how an Old School researcher would devise "correct" strategy for the game of football:

First, he'd conclude (wrongly) that each team performed the same over time (because of the use of the random number generator to simulate the game) -- all teams' statistics would be virtually the same.

Then, compiling and averaging out the results from millions and millions of simulated games, his strategy would recommend using a simple approach - using just one defensive formation that, over millions of downs, performed the

Is The Strategy You're Using Faulty?

best, versus all teams. No need to study opposing teams and fashioning a flexible and unique strategy for each, as is done in football today. Just one defense. The same would be true of his offensive team strategy: he'd average out the results of millions of simulated downs, and then, averaging out the numbers, choose just one strategy that statistically achieved the best results.

Ridiculous, right?

Or, if an Old School blackjack researcher were designing a battleship, he'd devise his anti-aircraft guns such that they would anticipate encountering a jet fighter going at the *average* speed of all jet fighters in existence. If one fighter flew at 200 miles an hour, another at 900 mph, the third at 1000, the guns, therefore, would be set to shoot down a plane going 700 mph.

That's *ridiculous*, right? But that's *exactly* the kind of "logic" that produced the concept of Basic Strategy!

Flawed? You bet!!!

For instance, answer this question: What's the difference between a dealer's up card of 6 that has a 10 in the hole, and a dealer's up card of 10 that has a 6 in the hole? *The answer is: nothing!!! So, you should play a 10 that has a 6 in the hole the same way you'd handle a 6 with a 10 in the hole!* In other words, taking a Basic Strategy approach versus that 10 as if it was much stronger than that 6 would result in your making the wrong card moves! Yet that's exactly what the methods of the 20th Century recommend.

Of course, you need the skill of determining what the hole card is likely to be and a good card analysis method (both of which are unique to my system) to move on to a more modern, more educated and more precise approach. (We'll take a look at all of this later on.) For now, the point I'm making here is: *make sure you're not using an antiquated system or one based upon faulty logic!*

Another Reason To Move Beyond The Old School Methods

A scientist should know how to research a subject; there are many ways you can go wrong, and before starting research, much thought needs to put into the procedure to be followed so that the study is valid.

In blackjack, such care was not taken when the research was done that led to the late-20th Century methods still prevalent today. Today, I specifically want to discuss why their failure to use real cards led to systems that will cost you in the way of potential winnings.

Think about it – if you wanted to study moon rocks, would you program your computer to *simulate* what you *think* moon rocks are, and then study your computer's *simulation*? Obviously, no!

So, why have blackjack researchers since 1960 been content with *simulating* blackjack with their computers' *random number generators* instead of using real cards, which do *not* play out randomly? Is it because they chose to take the easy way out? (It takes longer to properly study card behavior, of course, because it requires many months for real dealers to produce the data needed for a valid study.) Or were they so enamored of their machines that they didn't realize that computers could not and should not have been used to *create* their data?

By studying results produced randomly with their computers' random number generators, the Old School researchers -- unbeknownst to them I'm sure -- were actually studying *computer* behavior and not *card* behavior! Therefore, there are many things they missed and there are many ways their conclusions (and systems) are faulty as a result.

For example, my study into how shuffling rearranges the cards (in which I started with real cards, dealt, collected and shuffled by real casino dealers as they do at real casinos, then putting that real-world data into the computer to analyze) proved that *standardized casino shuffling does not change the order of the cards very much*. I also discovered never-before-known *repeating* phenomena that resulted from such shuffling.

These are discoveries from which you, the player, can profit. Yet the Old School researchers completely overlooked these, because they bypassed the dealing, card collection and shuffling processes by doing computer simulations instead of using real cards.

Interestingly enough, an Old School blackjack author who came to one of my book events in California admitted *he was aware that computer simulations produce faulty results, before he wrote his books based upon those simulations!* But he tried to minimize the damage by arguing that the shortcomings of doing things that way are inconsequential. Unfortunately for him, they're *not*.

Here's some of the many things the Old School researchers missed by doing computer simulations instead of using real cards in their studies:

New Ways To Win MORE At Blackjack

1. They failed to discover that *many aspects of the game are predictable*

2. They failed to discover that *the dealer's hole card can be identified with good accuracy*

3. They failed to discover *you can follow significant cards through a shuffle* (a practice now known as shuffle tracking)

4. They failed to discover *there's a way to cut the cards intelligently to bring back good cards or avoid bad ones*

5. They failed to discover that *you can determine whether good or bad cards are coming after a shuffle, and, therefore, know whether you should raise or lower your bet*

6. They failed to discover that *the cards stay very much the same after they're shuffled, leading to a predictability that tells you how to bet and whether or not you should stay at the table*

7. They failed to discover that *dealing brings cards separated slightly by shuffling back together*

8. They failed to discover *you can identify players' face-down cards at 1- and 2-deck tables with good accuracy*

9. They failed to discover *you can predict what your hit card will be with good accuracy*

   And that's just the tip of the iceberg. The point is – the Old School methods are based on faulty research and, in the long run, they'll cost you money!

How Good Is Card Counting?

Faulty and antiquated (nearly 50 years old), the myth is still being spread that card counting is the best way to win at blackjack. The truth is far different. Card counting was good for the times in which it was invented, but my more modern methods leave that approach in the dust.

Blackjack's first computer-research-generated books admitted that card counting was developed because its creators realized that their Basic Strategy approach did not produce very good results. Basic, they discovered, was only valid if the cards were balanced (that is, all cards were in the same proportion among the undealt pile as they were in an unopened deck -- each one accounting for 7.69% of the pile, except for the 10s, four times as numerous).

But, in reality, it is rare for the cards to be balanced. Therefore the need for something more accurate.

But, how much did card counting improve things?

Not so much. If you read *Bringing Down The House* (about those MIT students who claimed to have won millions playing as a team), they admitted that, using the popular Hi-Lo card counting system, they only got an additional edge of 2%. They also confessed that this was a paltry return for all of their efforts.

As a result, they had to take a high degree of risk by placing huge bets, in order to make the kind of money they wanted to make. Not a good thing to do for the average player.

The return you'd expect from most other card counting systems would be in a similar range. In other words, the much-touted card counting methods born of the 1950s and 60s didn't do much for players in the way of making the game more winnable.

Now, I did create my own card counting system in the 1980s – the All-Inclusive Card Counting System (where 2s through 7s count as +1, and 8s through 10s count as -1, and Aces are counted separately). But, in the years since, I've moved on to a whole new approach, because of the inadequacies of card counting, as an *approach*.

I know this sounds like sacrilege to some, but, really I don't understand why they'd be so narrow-minded as to cling to something so antiquated and hopeless. Why are they happy with returns of 2% (at best)? It's time to admit the Emperor has no clothes!

By calling a group of cards low cards and another group of cards high cards (each system defining these differently), you're placing vastly different cards together whose effect on your present and future are quite different. Plus, the end result – a number indicating the relative balance between the two groups – does not give you enough information.

Let's take the example on top of the next page, for instance. You're the player holding the 8 and the 3, in third base. Should you double?

How Good Is Card Counting?

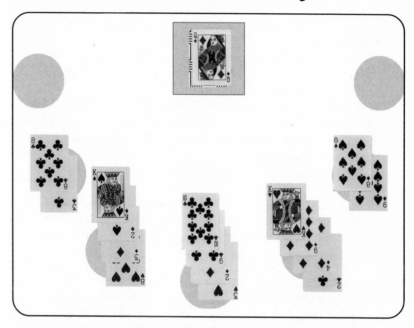

Most Old School Basic Strategists would say yes. They've been trained not to look at the cards and make intelligent decisions.

Let's see what card counters would say.

The Hi-Opt I and II, Revere Advanced +- and ITA methods tell you the count is zero at your turn. What does THAT tell you? Nothing! In fact, although a count of zero would make you think the cards are balanced, they're NOT! Aces and 5s through 7s are overdue – NONE were dealt. Now, the Hi-Lo, Revere Point Count and Revere Advanced Point Count say the count is +3; the Thorp Ultimate Count is +4. But, similarly, things are NOT positive here – with Aces overdue and 8s and 9s overplayed, the player is looking at the likelihood of double-digit losses ahead. In comparison, my All-Inclusive Card Counting System gives us a more accurate read on this situation: it gives you a count of -3. Low cards are overdue.

More to the point – should you double here? Even though my card counting system (and my system alone) gave us an important clue, card analysis yields the most accurate read on this situation:

Cards that would *hurt* you (5s-7s) are *overdue*, and most that would *help* you (8s, 9s and Aces) were *overplayed* (except for the 10s, which were only slightly underplayed). Now, let's analyze the *card flow* that led up to your turn. The cards you most wanted, 9s and 10s, were greatly overrepresented in that mix; *therefore they're less likely to come your way with your hit card!*

So, with you hit card likely to be a *bad* one, why double and be limited to that one when the dealer has such a strong up card? You should *NOT* double here. *Hitting* your hand is the smartest move.

This was just one example I could have shown you. I think you can see why card counting often gives you not only a fuzzy idea of what's going on...it also often misleads you.

The point is -- card counting is antiquated and bankrupt. The proof of the pudding is in the fact that card counting failed the average player -- it proved to be too difficult and too ineffective for most players. The number of players now availing themselves of any card counting system is minuscule -- probably less than 1%. At every book signing event and seminar I've done nationwide these past five years, I've asked the question: how many of you are card counters? Of the thousands of players I've met, well fewer than 1% said they had tried such a system, and even fewer were still using the card counting system they'd tried.

It's time for blackjack players to move on to something more modern and effective, such as the methods produced in my most recent computer research studies. These produce not only a higher winning rate vis a vis how often you'll come home a winner, they will increase the percentage of rounds you'll win at the table, and they will increase your gains -- the amount of money you will win on any winning day.

Homemade Card Strategies
&
Player Confusion About Stiffs

A man once interrupted one of my New York City area book events to announce:

"I *always stand on 16s against the dealer's 10!*"

He said it in a conspiratorial tone, the back of his hand up against the left corner of his mouth, as if this was priceless information that would be spoiled if too many people found out about it.

I responded quizzically, however.

"Why on earth would you do *that?*" I asked.

"Because I win *85% of the time, doing that!*" he shouted, while beating a hasty retreat into a nearby department store before I had a chance to enlighten this gentleman about the truth of the situation, which is far different than what he perceived it to be. (And yet, looking back on it, he was clearly uninterested in knowing the truth! How strange!)

What he said was *preposterous;* I hope you realize that.

(We'll examine this in a second.)

But, sadly, this gentleman is not alone. Surprisingly enough, lurking around every corner, it seems, is another player with another crazy, homemade theory on how to play stiffs. (Stiffs are hands of 12, 13, 14, 15 or 16 points, which bust more than any other point totals.)

For instance, there was a gal who, again, interrupted one of my book events, to tell everyone that she always *stands* on hands of 12 points versus the dealer's 2, because "the dealer busts *every* time!" (Try, on average, 35% of the time. But, she too, like the man I mentioned above, ran off before I could discuss the subject with her.)

Anyway, it's clear to me that a lot of players are totally thrown off by the problem of how to handle their stiff hands. (No wonder those hands are so often played *wrongly*!)

I've seen players stand on 16s versus the dealer's stronger up cards, in rounds where the dealer was undoubtedly going to reach a good score. I've seen players stand on 12s versus the dealer's weaker up cards in rounds where those up cards were likely to reach strong scores.

Ultimately, you will need to learn that all of the dealer's up cards have times when they are hard to beat, and other times when they are vulnerable to being beaten. Identifying these phases is key to knowing how to play any up card in any given round (in other words, you need some card analysis skills, so you know how the up card is likely to play out, based upon what cards have been dealt).

You should also familiarize yourself with each up card's *score profile* (my term), so you know their specific strengths and weaknesses. That's a term I invented to describe the percentage of times each up card, on average, reaches scores of 17, 18, 19, 20 and 21. (Did you know that each up card has a *different* score profile?!) I address these issues in *Blackjack The SMART Way* and *Cutting Edge Black-*

Homemade Card Strategies

jack, and I'll discuss them in later columns. My research into this has forced the blackjack world to reevaluate the relative player friendliness of each up card. (If the gal I referred to above had known her score profiles, she would never have been so bold as to say the dealer's 2 *always* busts!)

Nonetheless, in this column, let's examine the opinion of the man I mentioned at the start of this column, and see if he's right about how you should handle your hard hand total of 16 when the dealer shows a 10. (PLEASE NOTE: when I say a 10, of course, I mean a 10-point card, which includes the pips -- the cards that say "10" -- and the face cards.)

Let's assume you don't know yet how to determine what the dealer's hole card is. This is a powerful technique unique to my system, which allows you to make smarter card moves. After all, what is the difference between a dealer's 4 that sits on a hole card of 10, and a dealer's 10 that sits on a hole card of 4? Nothing! So, once you've learned how to estimate, with a high degree of certainty, what the hole card is, using my method, you'll be *standing* on your 16s versus the dealer's 10, when you know the hole card gives the dealer a stiff total! (In other words, a *beginner* looking at this problem will come to a *different* conclusion than a *more knowledgeable player* using my system would, because of a more limited scope of skills.)

So we don't get ahead of ourselves, let's look, in this column, at what's wisest for the player who has not yet mastered my more potent methods for beating the house. If you're that level of player, you'd first want to ask yourself: how often does the dealer's 10 bust, on average? You'd specifically want to know the rate at which the dealer's 10 busts *when the dealer does not have a blackjack* because you only play against the 10 when there is no Ace in the hole. My research indicates the dealer 10's bust rate, when we know the dealer has no blackjack, is 22% (about two percentage points higher than the Old School books say).

So, look at what you've just learned. By *standing* on your

16 versus that 10, you will only win when the dealer busts. Therefore, since the 10 in that case busts just 22% of the time, you will *lose* **78 out of every 100 hands!** Not a pretty picture. (And certainly not a reality that bears out what the man at the book event had said!)

Let's look at this from a different angle, from the point of view of your **overall losses.** If you stood on your hands of 16 points when facing the dealer's 10, your **overall losses,** over time, would be **56%.** (To determine your overall losses, you subtract your loss rate from your win rate. In this case: 22% wins - 78% losses = **-56%.**)

Now, if you had the option of *surrendering* (which is not allowed at all casinos), you could hold down your overall losses to **50%.** (To surrender, you simply say "surrender" at your turn, and the dealer confiscates *half* of your bet.) So, *that's your very best option.* (An option, I'm sure that man at the book event didn't even realize players have, at some casinos.)

But what if the casino doesn't allow surrender?

Then, you should *hit* your 16. Granted, you'd bust in more than 60 of every 100 rounds (and you'd lose in other rounds due to the dealer outscoring you), but your **overall losses** over time (with *wins* taken into account) *would be held to slightly less than 55%.*

By *hitting*, you'd lose 74.44% of the hands. You'd also push 5.99% of the time. But you'd also *win* 19.57% of the time. To figure out your overall losses, the equation would look like this: **19.57% wins - 74.44% losses = -54.87%.**

So, to summarize, when holding a hard-hand total of 16 points versus the dealer's 10, you'll be a loser no matter what you do. In this type of predicament, you'd be smart to make the move that cuts your losses to a bare minimum.

It may seem like splitting hairs when it comes down to choosing between hitting and standing in this example, but if you can win 1% more hands by *hitting* rather than *stand-*

ing (assuming surrender is not allowed), then that's the way to go. It means more money in your pocket.

By the way, in this column we took a *global* look, a more old-fashioned way of analyzing the card situation presented. However, once you start using my more modern, more precise methods, as a more advanced player, you'll have more skills with which you can analyze the specific reality you're facing in any given round and cut your losses even further. We'll explore that, in the very next column.

The point of this column is that you cannot simply throw caution to the wind and make up your own way to play blackjack if you want to be successful -- that is, unless you've done carefully-planned and executed research that began with the exacting casino-style standardized shuffling, dealing and collecting of cards (over an impossibly long period) and concluded with a proper analysis of your results.

The mathematics behind well-researched strategies is more complicated than you would imagine -- starting with the collection of accurate data, the proper analysis of that data, and then the application of the proper equations applicable to each situation (if equations are called for) or the proper conclusions regarding what you've observed.

OK, so if you accept that premise and (if, like 99.999% of all blackjack players, you'd rather not set aside the next three years of your life doing quality blackjack research), then I think you'll be excited to learn of the many unique discoveries I've made through my many years of doing research. These have led to my creating many fabulous new *methods* from which you can profit greatly (as many thousands of players already have).

Blackjack's Most Misunderstood Problem: How To Play Your 15s & 16s

The question I am most frequently asked is "when should I hit a 15 or 16?" The question is usually punctuated by a laugh, indicating the questioner has been frustrated in his attempts to get a good answer to this problem from the methods of the past.

In fact, the problem of how to handle your worst stiffs is probably the most misunderstood issue in blackjack. Hands of 15 and 16 points are, in the long run, definitely losing hands; but, with finesse, you can cut your losses.

Old School Basic Strategist fanatics – and, sadly, there are still too many of them – respond to this question by whipping out antiquated statistics that are based on faulty premises. No matter what card imbalance reflected in the cards that have been dealt, they give you one simple solution to this complex problem: *hit!*

But, as you've learned in prior columns, the Basic Strategy method *failed* in its woeful attempt to provide a winning approach to the game. So, that's not the way to go. (Basic

Blackjack's Most Misunderstood Problem: 15s & 16s

Strategy's inventors *admitted* its shortfalls. As Lawrence Revere wrote in *Playing Blackjack As A Business*: "If you play Basic Strategy...and play *perfectly* you will *break even*" [my italics and underlining]. But you don't want to just *break even,* do you? You want a strategy to *win!*)

To play the most precise game, you need to learn the skill of card analysis and react to the realities at hand.

Here are two questions you can ask of any hand you hold in order to become a better player:

1. What hit cards do I need (if any) to reach an acceptable score, and are they in good supply (based upon the card imbalances at hand)?

2. What score do I need to make my hand competitive with the dealer's? (You need to assess whether the dealer is likely to bust, or, if not, what *score* the dealer is likely to arrive at. Part of the process requires a complete understanding of up card behavior – a topic I've covered and will continue to cover in my columns.)

For example, what do you need when holding a hand of 15 or 16 points? Of the 13 different types of cards, only six would be of any assistance to your 15 (the Ace, 2, 3, 4, 5 and 6), and only five would be of any help to your 16 (the Ace, 2, 3, 4, and 5). That's a minority of cards, which is why your position, most times, is a losing proposition.

But, wait! Even though the Ace wouldn't bust you, it wouldn't give your 15 or 16 a winning score, would it? So your situation is that much more tenuous.

Plus, what card you need depends upon what the dealer's up card is, and what the likely hole card is. Even if you know you'll probably draw to an acceptable score, you need to know if your score would likely beat the dealer's.

Now, I'm not suggesting you can achieve 100% accuracy in making card moves. It would be very rare that you'd get down so far in the cards where you knew the exact identity of all the undealt cards AND where they were all one type of card. Short of that, you can never predict exactly what card is coming next.

What you can do, however, is play the percentages, based upon an intelligent assessment of the mathematical probabilities you face.

OK, so now you know:

1. You need to analyze the cards – the cards that have been dealt so far, as well as the hand you hold – to determine whether the card you need to achieve a good score is likely to come with the next hit card.

2. Then, you need to assess how your likely score would stack up against the dealer's likely result.

So, how does this work?

Say the dealer's up card is a 10, and you've determined through card analysis that the hole card is most likely a 3, 4, 5, or 6; then, you'd *stand* on your 15 or 16 – just as you would if that likely *low* card in the hole were instead the up card. This situation would occur, for instance, if no 3s, 4s, 5s or 6s had been dealt by your turn, at a table with four or more players; or, if way too few of these cards had been dealt by your turn (vis a vis the proportions in which you'd expect to find them, as in a deck of cards).

If, however, the dealer in this example likely has a 10 in the hole; 10s are overdue at your turn AND all of the 5s and 6s have been played out, you'd be crazy not to *surrender* your 15 (if that option is available). The same would be true of your 16 if all the 4s and 5s had been dealt prior to your turn. (You tell the dealer "surrender!" and you get to keep half your bet.)

Incidentally – along these lines – if you're *really* serious about wanting to make the most of your 15s and 16s, then you'll seek out casinos that offer surrender, whenever possible! Even beginners can make an extra 3% in gains by

Blackjack's Most Misunderstood Problem: 15s & 16s

surrendering according to my Basic Strategy dictates. (Please understand that my Basic Strategy approach is meant only as an entry-level method, for *beginners* only.* See chart on page 79.)

Another example – the dealer's up card is a 7, and you're holding a 16 in the last round of action at either a 1- or 2-deck table. Most of the 2s, 3s, 4s, 5s, 6s, 7s and 10s have been dealt, as have ALL of the Aces; *few* 8s or 9s have appeared. In this case, *standing* is smartest. The probability is the hole card will be one of the under-represented cards (8s and 9s), giving the dealer a likely 15 or 16. True too, your hit card would likely bust you. Basic Strategists should understand this concept: when the dealer has a stiff, you stand on stiffs (this was, after all, the concept behind their approach versus the dealer's 4 through 6, was it not?).

This new and more accurate approach might seem over-whelming when presented in part in a brief column, but trust me – I've tested it by computer and at the blackjack table, and it *works*. You'd do better to read the complete details in one of my books, of course, if you want to fully understand what's involved in playing blackjack with *precision*.

All that is required of you is that you train yourself to be observant, you learn how to quickly analyze the cards, you familiarize yourself with up card behavior, and you play the percentages properly.

*Later on, I'll have you refer back to my Basic Strategy in guiding you toward making more precise card moves through my Ducks & Bucks method. I did this purely so that the Ducks & Bucks concept would be easier for you to learn and apply, because Basic is so familiar to you. As you will see, though, you'll be using the Basic Strategy dictates in a very unorthodox way.

On Splitting Aces: Never Say Always

Here's one of my bugaboos: the notion that players should *always* split Aces. I was on a gaming talk show in Las Vegas, on KRLV, whose host was a supposed expert (the truth is -- I know him personally -- he's not even a player, let alone an expert), and this guy was flabbergasted when I informed him Aces should NOT always be split. (The galling thing is that I later saw this guy on a cable TV show, pretending to be a blackjack authority.)

It amazes me how many so-called experts tell players always to split their Aces, when even the designers of the world's first computer-driven blackjack strategies of the 20th Century made it clear that this advice was only perti-nent to those who played according to some Basic Strategy formula. Today's "experts" should go back and read the books of the 1960s and 1970s -- the books they say they revere -- a bit more carefully.

It's one thing for players to harbor this misconception; it's another thing when supposed experts espouse and perpetu-ate this loser's truism (which, sadly, occurs all too frequently -- I just read one the other day).

On Splitting Aces

If a player is a *beginner*, that's one thing. My Basic Strategy formula -- as all Basic Strategies that I know of -- calls for splitting Aces at all times. But I make it clear that Basic Strategy is only for *beginners*.

Make no mistake. That advice does not apply to non-beginners. *It is not always smart to split Aces.*

Why anyone might perceive this as being controversial is beyond me. This truth has been known for more than 40 years.

Go back to Edward Thorp's *Beat The Dealer*, first published in 1961. This book introduced the (now-antiquated) late-20th Century approach to blackjack (which I now refer to as the Old School approach). Simply open to the middle of this book (where you'll find the strategy charts, on card stock), and look at Thorp's Ten Count Strategy. Whereas he would have had you splitting 8s up to and including the dealer's up card of 9 without exception, his advice on splitting Aces is another matter. In that case, he warns you that there are situations *versus every dealer up card* where you should *not* split them, and he goes into *specifics*.

The same goes for Lawrence Revere's Ten Count Strategy. See page 108, for instance, in *Playing Blackjack As A Business*, first published in 1969. He details when you should not split Aces versus the dealer's *8 through Ace*.

There are good reasons why you might *not* want to split your Aces.

At most casinos, you are only given just one hit card upon each split Ace. That's a *severe* limitation. This is especially true when you're facing the dealer's strongest up cards. *If your Aces receive anything but 9s and 10s, you'll likely end up a loser*. What sense does it make to split your Aces if you are aware you are likely to be dealt low cards upon each Ace and wind up with two weak hands, both of which are likely to lose?

So, then, how does a player know when splitting Aces is

wise?

If you use my All-Inclusive Card Counting System (where 2s through 7s are counted as +1, and 8s through 10s as -1), you'd have a real good idea of how your Aces might fare when split. In *Blackjack The SMART Way*, I recommend that you NOT split your Aces once the count reaches -4 or below, when facing the dealer's 9, 10 or Ace. Just *hit* them. A pair of Aces, in fact, does quite well when *hit*.

If you move on to the more modern approach introduced in *Cutting Edge Blackjack* (involving what I call *Strategic Card Analysis*), you'll *avoid* splitting Aces when 9s and 10s are depleted *and* the dealer is likely to achieve a strong score (no matter what the up card). Predicting the dealer's outcome is beyond the scope of this column, but, suffice it to say, this can be done, with a very good degree of accuracy.

In conclusion, the general principle goes something like this: *when low cards are likely to fall on your Aces and the dealer is likely NOT to bust, you'd be crazy to split them.*

On
Splitting 10s

Sharon Sweeney, publisher of the Colorado Gambler, had a question for me: what do you think about players who split 10s?

If I were being glib, I might answer, "Not much." But, actually, the answer is not as cut-and-dried as you would think.

In fact, one question I like to ask players who come to my book events is about this topic. One approach I take is to ask them: "Do you think Lawrence Revere (author of the blackjack bestseller *Playing Blackjack As A Business*) would ever recommend splitting 10s?" (I ask them about Revere, because he's an author who's generally well-respected.)

Those who have read Revere always laugh at that question, as if it's ridiculous -- which is precisely how I want them to react. Because, if they think he was dead set against splitting 10s, then they didn't read Revere closely enough.

See page 149 in his book. He talks about recommending

"unusual plays" with the Advanced Point Count method he'd recently developed. "Some of the unusual plays," he wrote, "are...split two tens vs. 7 or 8."

Revere was a player, and a smart man. When first published (in 1969), his book represented a step forward in blackjack thinking. Although my system is based upon a more modern understanding of card behavior, I, too, have found that, on *rare* occasions - I repeat, *RARE* occasions — splitting 10s versus the dealer's weaker up cards (including the 7 and 8) makes good sense...but, is it *wise?* By that I mean, even if you're an advanced player who can, with my methods, predict with good accuracy when you'd get two winning hands by splitting your 10s, would the added income offset the negative reaction you'd provoke at the table?

Now, in most other situations, I've counseled players to ignore the criticism of other players. But, in this case, the effect might be to scare away your fellow players. You would likely find yourself alone at the table for the following rounds, after all the other players scattered to different tables. This would be very bad for your ability to win future hands. You don't want to play head-on versus the dealer (in spite of what some others have told you). And changes in the number of betting spots being played might very well affect you adversely - even if just one or two players leave. (I'll cover these issues in a later column.)

Plus - for all but the most advanced players — splitting 10s is a *foolish* move. A player hard hand total of 20 wins nearly 75% of the time. Split those 10s, and only one of thirteen possible hit cards (8%) - the Ace - will better your score, and only four of thirteen (31%) possible hit cards would give your split 10s a 20. *Seven* of 13 possible hit cards (54%) - the 2, 3, 4, 5, 6, 7 and 8 - would give you stiffs or weak scores. Even if you received a 9, you'd be greatly reducing your chances of a win (player 19s win 59% of the time).

So - a word to the wise: keep those 10s together.

How To Find A Good Table

So you've arrived at a casino and you go to the nearest available table and sit down...Right?

Wrong. If you're doing that, then you've not mastered the crucial skill of picking a good table.

If you're guilty of this, you're not alone. Few players I've met on my book and seminar tours are aware that they can develop the ability to discern which tables offer them the best probability of winning.

You can be a crackerjack player but if you don't have this basic skill your winning rate is going to suffer; in fact, you'll probably wind up a *loser*. Being without it is akin to buying a performance car and then sitting in the back seat when you're supposed to be driving.

All tables are not created equal. Some hold promise. Some do not. You need to learn to be discriminating.

The First Rule

Rule #1 in finding a good table is a very simple one that will serve you well: *ask the players how the action's been!*

(Now this may sound obvious, but very, very few players do this!) This tactic will uncover a host of problems.

The Dealer Factor

For instance, I recently sat down at a blackjack table next to a friend, and when I asked him how it was going he replied: "Not so good. This dealer always *kills* me!"

"Thanks," I replied, immediately getting up from that table. Upon seeing me leave, he looked perplexed. Looking at him staying there made me just as perplexed. Didn't he understand that he had the right and the physical ability to get up and find a better table, with a better dealer? Didn't he realize that there undoubtedly was a *reason* why he didn't win against that dealer ever? *Hello!*

One significant determinant of your success at any table is the *dealer* who's there! So, if the dealer is known as a player-killer, *don't play at his or her table!*

Other dealers to avoid include ones I call Quick Ricks, who speed up the action to a ridiculously fast pace, and Bigmouth Berthas, whose rudeness is a distraction.

Think BEFORE Sitting Down

Your ears can often be your guide in finding a good table. As you approach a table, *listen to the chatter*.

If you hear the players complaining about how often they've been losing, walk away. "Not again!" is a familiar refrain you'll hear at bad tables.

Bad tables are often so because the *mix of cards* is bad. (Ask any poker player about bad cards!) For instance, if the shuffle produces a mix where many of the cards fall into a high-low-high-low pattern, that's a killer mix, producing many player stiffs and a high player busting rate. If you see that, don't sit down at the table!

Also, don't fall for the commonly-held myth that you can change the order of the cards for the better by joining a table. Trust me -- I've done the research. That won't

How To Find A Good Table

happen. If the cards are bad when you arrive, they'll be bad when you've joined the table to play.

My most recent computer research project proved that shuffling does not change the order of the cards very much. In addition, I've identified repeating phenomena that result from standardized casino shuffling which includes one I call "orbiting associations," where huge blocks of cards appear together in the same round, from shuffle to shuffle. Your joining the table won't change the order of the cards for the better with large-scale patterns like that going on.

To spot the bad card mixes, simply use your eyes and your powers of observation. Watch a few rounds of action. *If you witness EVERYONE at the table lose hand after hand, don't sit down.*

It's unusual for *everyone* at a table to lose in any one round, and it's even more unusual for that to continue for any length of time. That might be a sign the mix of cards is bad. Or it could be something more sinister. Whatever the reason (it's of no concern to you), it's a bad sign.

Penetration And True Penetration

Let's talk about two more factors: penetration and true penetration.

Penetration is the percentage of cards the dealer blocks off when putting the cut card in after the shuffling process. (If the dealer places the card exactly in the middle, you're getting 50% *penetration*, for instance.)

This helps determine how many cards will be dealt before the next shuffle – and the more cards, the better. The more cards you see, the more accurate you'll be in determining what cards are likely to come next, and therefore, what your best card move will be under the circumstances.

If the dealer's placing of the reshuffle card causes players to get significantly less than 60% penetration, move to a better table (or casino!). Dealers sometimes determine how much penetration you get, but often that's decided by casino policy. This often varies from table to table, too -- determined by the number of decks in the game and the minimum bet required.

Now, *True Penetration* is my term for *the exact number of cards you'll be dealt between shuffles,* on average. This depends primarily upon the number of players at the table.

I've shown in my most recent computer study that, the more players at the table, the more cards you'll see per round as well as between shuffles. So, in choosing a table, *the more players at the table, the better,* for this factor alone.

Crowded Tables Are Often Better Tables

There are two other reasons you should seek out crowded tables:

Number one, as I pointed out in my audio book, *Richard Harvey's Blackjack PowerPrep Session: "Don't forget - it's often the crowded tables that are doing well. Think about it. No one is likely to leave a good table, when they're winning."* (Conversely, if you see players scattering from a table, that's often a sign of a *bad* table.)

Number two, as I revealed in *Cutting Edge Blackjack: your probability of winning goes up significantly with each additional betting spot that's being played! In fact, if you play the dealer head-on, you're looking at double-digit losses over time.*

Other Factors

Other factors to look for in choosing a table:

Look for any unusual restrictions that would hurt your ability to win. For instance, if you cannot double after splitting, or if you can only double down on hands of 10 or 11 points, try to find tables without this restriction. The latter restriction alone results in a 3% player disadvantage. Also, if the maximum bet allowed is below what you'd like to bet, that will potentially cut into your earnings.

How To Find A Good Table

Tables within casinos of varying numbers of decks and minimum bets often vary with regard to restrictions and player options. Find a table that won't cramp your potential.

Some tables might offer special advantages; *surrender*, for example. That's where you're allowed to fold and keep half your bet. This is a very powerful tool, if you know when to use it.

"No Mid-Point Entry Tables" keep out the harmful players who come in for a hand or two of action between shuffles and then leave, often spoiling the flow of cards. These are great, if all the other considerations are also player-friendly.

The Number of Decks in Play

If you have a choice, play at tables with the fewest decks in play (unless, of course, if there are severe restrictions; a 1-deck table, for example, is no good if they only deal one round of action). Every good book in print since 1961 has warned you that each deck added to the mix increases the odds in favor of the house. (I'll discuss this from another angle in the next column.)

...And that's just a taste of what goes into picking a good table. What you need to understand is that, if you go about this wisely, it can improve your bottom line significantly!

Shoe
vs.
Pitch Games

I was on Mike Rosen's talk show on KOA-AM in Denver a couple of years ago, and a player phoned in to ask me what the difference was between a 1-deck and a 6-deck game.

"There are many differences," I told him. "For instance, if you're playing a 1 deck game and you've seen four Aces in the first round, how many Aces are likely to come in the next round?"

"None!" he replied, laughing.

"Right, that's obvious, isn't it?" I said. "Now, if you've seen four Aces in the first round of a 6 deck game, how many are coming in the next round?"

"Well," he said, "I don't know!"

"Right," I answered. "There are 20 Aces left! It's hard to predict how many might come in the next round, isn't it?"

And that's one of the major differences between pitch games (1 and 2 deck games) and shoe games (games

Shoe vs. Pitch Games

involving 4 or more decks, dealt from a "shoe" or card holder). Shoe games do not offer the player the same level of predictability that pitch games do. That's one reason why – *no matter what system you use* – *you will never be able to win as much at shoe games, over time, as you will with pitch games.* Pitch games afford a higher level of predictability, which gives the player much more precision in making intelligent card moves and bets.

But, of course, that's why shoe games were introduced in the 1960s – to make it harder for players to win. EVERY good book on blackjack tells you the same: your disadvantage versus the house goes up with every deck added to the game.

One other difference I want to explore with you today (and I don't know of anyone who has pointed this out before), which the graphic example on the top of the following page points out.

Look at it and ask yourself this question: Is this an example from a pitch game or a shoe game?

It's definitely a situation you could only encounter in a shoe game. There are *four* 2♣s! This would have to represent a 4-deck or higher game.

Now, notice what the first baseman got. An ELEVEN card hand! You would *never* see that in a 1-deck game. And it would be EXCEEDINGLY rare to see that in a 2-deck game. In shoe games, however, with so many more low cards available, these hands would show up much more.

Plus, notice that the average number of cards per hand (up to the third baseman's turn) in this particular example is SIX cards! In a 1-deck game, that average would be more like THREE cards. I'm not suggesting the overall average number of cards at a multideck table would be six, but, as you can see, in individual rounds, it certainly can -- very unlike a 1-deck game.

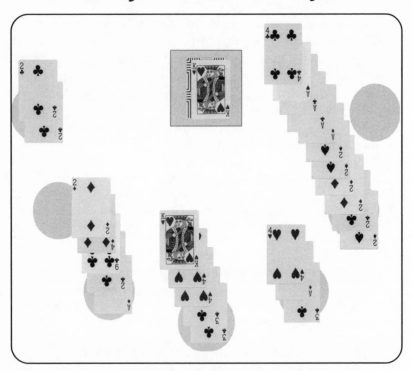

In other words, *the card composition of your hands varies in a 6-deck game versus a 1-deck game.* With so many more low cards available in the 6-deck game (144, versus 24 in a 1-deck game), hands can get really wild looking! *With a poor mix of cards many of those low cards might wind up in clumps (as in the above example), which causes the dealer's probability of busting to go down significantly (and your chances of winning, as well).*

In these respects, the 6-deck game is a completely differ-ent animal than the 1-deck game, and it's not to my liking.

And, add two more decks, and you can imagine how much worse an 8-deck game is. You can experience killer streaks of low cards in that game that never seem to end.

...So a player's realities are very different in pitch games vs. shoe games. Pitch games are your best bet, every time.

What To Do When A Player Leaves The Table

You're sitting at a table and one player leaves. What should you do? Pick the correct response or responses from any of the following possible answers:

1. Ignore it. It doesn't mean anything.

2. Leave the table. That will mess up everything.

3. Lower your bet. Play it cautiously.

4. Raise your bet. The cards might become lucky.

5. Take an extra betting spot, and try to keep things stable.

The most important thing you should take away from this column is that *you must never ignore the fact that a player has left the table*. There are a number of reasons why. My latest computer research project revealed that *the number of players at the table affects your probability of winning*. In sum, *the more crowded the table, the better your odds of winning*. Therefore, *if a player leaves, your odds of winning just went down* (in the long run). So, how should you react? In cases where you're *losing*, you should get up and go find a better table. For example, if you're at a 4-player table, you're not doing that well and a player leaves, you leave. Your probability of winning just plunged to an even worse (and unacceptable) level, and taking an extra betting spot is inadvisable here. That's because: a) as my recent computer research has proven, a player's overall likelihood of winning doesn't reach a positive level until there are *six* players at the table; and, b) if a player leaves and you take an extra betting spot, the effect will only be to perpetuate the bad cycle of cards you've been experiencing (and the bad cards the player who left was undoubtedly experiencing).

There are times, however, when you should take an extra betting spot when a player leaves your table. My research into card behavior proved that standardized casino dealer shuffling does not change the order of the cards very much. In fact, I discovered many *repeating* phenomena that result. One such phenomenon is *betting spot repetition*. *Each betting spot tends to get the same small repeating group of cards over a good number of shuffles — if the number of players remains the same.*

Therefore, if you've been on a good winning streak and someone leaves the table, taking an extra betting spot would keep the number of betting spots the same and, therefore, would likely keep your winning streak alive. (I call that extra bet a *placemaker bet*.) You'd then place higher bets on the spot that was winning for you than on the spot that essentially took over the less desirable cards from the player who left. Other situations call for you to simply play more cautiously. If a player leaves and no one takes an extra betting spot, understand that the flow of cards will change, and you've entered a period of uncertainty. Lower your bet until you see how your betting spot now performs.

Let's take an example from my research card runs. I dealt the same cards to various numbers of players, to see how things might change. In one 6-player situation of approximately one hours' playing time, the first baseman had won only 34% of the hands and the second baseman had won 45%

of the hands. If you were the second baseman, your table winning percentage as I call it, 45%, is only slightly below neutral (in other words, you're roughly even in wins versus losses). If you then chose to stay at the table when a player left -- since you're neither winning nor losing -- your best bet would be to lower your outlay to the minimum allowed table bet. Let's see how you'd then fare. I replayed the same cards to a 5-player situation, simulating the loss of a player. Guess what? The first baseman did much better, winning 43% of the time, and the second baseman (you) did much *worse*, winning just 36% of the time.

Things do change with the loss of a player and you'd better be ready to adjust to a new reality. Either leave, take another betting spot, or lower your bet to the minimum, depending on the scenario.

At the very least, when a player leaves, please recognize that you need to readjust your understanding of what the cards are telling you. If you're at a table with 7 players, for instance, approximately 22 cards will be dealt per round on average, *seven* of those likely to be 10-point cards. If a player who was playing two betting spots then leaves, things will change. You're now at a table with just 5 players. Now, just 16 cards will be dealt per round on average, *five* of those likely to be 10-point cards.

Why does this matter? An accurate read on probabilities comes from your recognition of what imbalances are in play. If seven 10s are dealt at a 7-player table, that's normal. If seven are dealt at a 5-player table, that's above normal; it signals a card imbalance, a surplus of tens dealt. You're then less likely to get a 10 if you need one. What I'm saying is, when a player leaves, the significance of what the cards are telling you changes. It calls for you to make a mental note to change the way you interpret what's on the table.

Taking into account the advent of a player leaving the table and reacting to it properly is just one of many widely unrecognized factors that go into becoming a winner.

Win More By Sitting In The Right Seat

One of the questions I'm asked most often is: *Where should I sit at the blackjack table? Is there one seat that's better than the others?*

The answer is: yes, there is one seat that's better than the rest. And by sitting in that seat, you can significantly increase your odds of winning!

But, what seat would that be? (Even if you *think* you know the answer, I'm about to show you something new that will knock your socks off!)

I've had some players venture a guess that first base is the best place to sit (that's the seat of the player whose turn is first). That's actually the *worst* seat to sit in, for a number of reasons.

Number one, the first baseman's turn comes up immediately after the first two cards are dealt. In other words, the player in that seat is under *pressure* to make a quick decision as to how best to play their hand. Why would you want

Win More By Sitting In The Right Seat

to put yourself under such pressure?

Plus, most players need a certain amount of time to make up their minds as to how to handle their hands. At first base, most players feel they need to make moves in haste; in haste, players wind up making a higher percentage of bad moves than if they took their time.

Number two, the first baseman sees the least amount of cards of any player before making his or her move. This is especially a drawback at 1- and 2-deck tables, where many players have yet to decide whether to stand or make a move, therefore negating the first baseman's ability to use my system for identifying what the other players' first cards are -- whether facedown or held in their hands (see *Cutting Edge Blackjack* for full details, or my column on this topic later in this book).

How does this differ from the situation the third baseman faces? Whereas 20 or more cards are likely to be dealt (and *known*, with a good deal of accuracy, using my method of identifying those cards) before the third baseman's move at a 7-player table, the first baseman would only be able to make out the dealer's up card and the cards of the few players who were quick enough to indicate, through body language or the placing of their cards under their chips, whether or not they wanted to stand.

The third baseman also has the benefit of seeing the faceup hit cards players take before his or her turn. No such cards are on the table before the first baseman's turn.

Your Winning Potential Goes Up From First to Third Base

I'm making a very important point here. Granted, it pertains especially to players who've learned to analyze the cards to make the smartest moves.

What I'm saying is that -- *if a player knows how to do card analysis -- his or her likelihood of winning increases statistically the closer he or she gets to third base.* As you will see in the dramatic example ahead, *a player's read on what move is smartest increases linearly with accuracy as you go around the table.*

Once you become a good card analyst, you'll realize how much information you can gain from reading the cards. The more cards that have been dealt before your turn, the better able you will be to predict how well the dealer is likely to do in the current round, as well as you. Therefore, the first baseman and those who sit near to that seat are handicapped by a lack of information, and vice versa, as you get closer to third base.

In other words, *the third baseman has the greatest potential to achieve the highest percentage of wins and the greatest gains.* (By "wins" I mean *the number of rounds in which the player beats the dealer*; by the word "gains" I mean *the amount of money the player walks away with at the end, above and beyond what the player brought to the table*).

Let's play out the round below and see how this works.

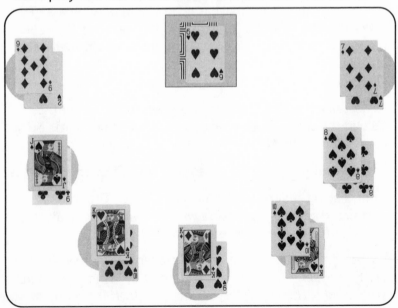

Win More By Sitting In The Right Seat

If you were sitting in first base, would you split those 7s? (Let's pretend you *know* what the other players hold. Normally at a 1-deck table, those cards would be held in players' hands and would be hidden. Then again, if you've read *Cutting Edge Blackjack*, you'd know my method of figuring out the identity of those cards, so you *would* know what they are!)

With the information at hand, most first basemen would split the 7s.

HOWEVER, *look at how the cards played out by the third baseman's turn*, in the graphic below! Would you, the first baseman, now knowing what the third baseman knows, now choose to split your 7s? Also, would a smart third baseman double on his 2♥-9♦? The answer to both questions should

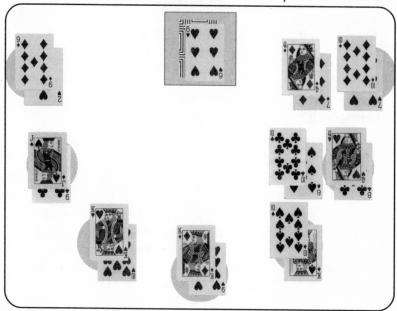

be: *No!*

The third baseman, having read *Cutting Edge Blackjack*, knows that the hole card with this card imbalance is a lot less likely than normal to be either a 10-pointer (which would give the dealer the most bustable total, 16) or a 9 (which would give the dealer the second most bustable total, 15).

How do we know this? By the third baseman's turn, *ten 10s were dealt*; that's *three* above average for *an entire seven-player round!* Also, *three of the four 9s were dealt!* The undealt cards, therefore are now unusually rich in low cards AND Aces (which would be of great help to the dealer in scoring).

Plus, my research shows that when the dealer's 6 is NOT likely sitting on a 9 or 10, it busts just 25% over time. In other words, it acts more like the dealer's *8!* A pair of 7s is a weak hand; you shouldn't split them when the dealer is this strong!

In addition, a smart third baseman, realizing the chances of getting a 9 or 10 here is so small, and the dealer's likelihood of scoring so high, would just *hit* the 2♥-9♦.

All of which proves that a first baseman can never get as good a read on the probabilities as the *third* baseman, and, therefore, has a lower winning potential.

So, for all of the reasons mentioned above, you'd be wise to sit at or near third base!

Of Course, Beginners Will Not Benefit As Much

Again, the benefits of sitting in third base primarily go to the players who know a *highly accurate, modern card analysis method* (such as my Card Observation method in *Blackjack The SMART Way* or Strategic Card Analysis method in *Cutting Edge Blackjack*). And that's a big *if*.

If you're simply playing according to someone's Basic Strategy formula instead of looking at what's been dealt and then reacting appropriately to the specific card imbalances you're facing, then it doesn't matter much what seat you sit in vis a vis your winning rate. A Basic Strategy player will gain more time to *think* by sitting in or near third base, but he or she won't gain any other advantage.

This should give you the motivation to learn how to analyze the cards. It's not very difficult once you understand the principles. Players of all levels can do it.

Another Reason Not To Sit In First Base

In his book, *How to Detect Casino Cheating at Blackjack*, former Nevada Gaming official Bill Zender also warns you not to sit in first base. He had observed certain types of scams by cheating dealers that were set up and designed solely for the first basemen. In other words, in his opinion, it's easier for cheating dealers to rip off the first baseman.

One Reason NOT To Sit At Third Base, However

So, sitting in first base (I'm sounding like a bad George Bush Sr. impressionist) is bad. That's baaaaad.

But, there's one wrinkle. You should not sit in third base if you're an absolute beginner.

Why?

Because many players believe that the third baseman has a direct influence on the dealer's outcome. More to the point: they feel a beginner louses up their odds of winning by making bad moves that enable the dealer to reach a score more than the dealer should. This feeling is largely unwarranted; but it results in beginners getting a lot of heat – stares and pointed criticism – when they sit in third base.

So, if you're relatively new to the game, don't sit in third base; sit as near to third base as possible. Players to the right of the third baseman aren't subjected to the kind of scrutiny that can make the third base position a hot seat.

...All of this is pretty mind blowing, isn't it?

Can Bad Players Mess Things Up At A Table?

One of the most frequent questions I get asked is: do bad players mess up the action?

Old School blackjack writers give this knee-jerk answer: *That's ridiculous! Bad players can't affect you at all!*

I respectfully disagree.

First of all, let's define what type of *bad players* we're talking about. Unfortunately, most players are not all that good.

There are players who play according to the Old School methods of the 1950s and 60s. They are operating on false assumptions, as I've pointed out in my books and columns. The ways of the past are faulty and antiquated. Yet this defines most blackjack players of today. So, in a sense, these players are playing badly; at least, they're not playing as well as they could with more modern methods. But I'm not referring to them when I refer to "bad players" in this column.

Can Bad Players Mess Things Up At A Table?

Then there are players who haven't bothered to learn much about the game, akin to skier wannabes who buy equipment and take to the slopes without taking lessons – these players often purchase basic strategy charts and go off ill-informed and half-cocked, without realizing they're going to fall on their faces.

Yet, these players, though ill-informed and under-prepared, are not the type of bad players I'm going to warn you about.

The players I'm saying are worth taking note of as "bad players" are the ones who are especially bad -- the ones who have absolutely no clue as to what to do, and, if they've learned anything at all, they've forgotten, and they make stupid moves based upon hunches. These are the ones asking the dealer and fellow players how to play. These are the ones standing on 15s and 16s against the dealer's 10 and Ace, for no reason. These are the ones who hit their 15s and 16s against the dealer's 4 through 6, for no reason. These are the ones hitting their 17s and splitting their 10s, again, for no reason. They are the players who make *all* of their moves for no apparent reason.

Why do these players louse things up?

Number one, they're a major distraction. Any major distraction at the table will cause you to lose concentration and therefore make mistakes of your own.

Number two, these players undoubtedly will make you angry and, if you're emotional, you will not be in the right frame of mind to make intelligent decisions.

OK, so those are the reasons why especially bad players mess things up on a *visceral* level. These are reason enough to avoid the tables where they're playing.

But, there are more important reasons to bypass or leave tables where there are really bad players.

Some of these bad players are actually *shills* -- casino employees who are pretending to be players. So, if you witness an especially bad player, you (at the very least) need to immediately determine whether they're a shill or not. Shills usually sit in third base (the seat of the player whose turn is last), and their job is to mess up the action for the players, in favor of the dealer. Not every casino employs shills, and encountering shills is not a common occurrence, but, if you play as much as I do, you will run into them sooner or later. Without going into details, if there's a player constantly making ridiculous moves (like splitting 10s or standing on 12s versus the dealer's 10), who obviously doesn't care when they lose, and when their crazy moves consistently result in the dealer getting great scores of 20 and 21, then you've probably found a shill. The solution? Leave that table. (For details, read Chapter 11 of *Blackjack The SMART Way*.)

I recently had the experience of being at a great 1-deck table, where most of us were winning. In comes a player, bringing the total number of players to seven. In that case, the casino's policy was to shuffle the cards after providing players with just one round of action -- a terrible situation that calls for your leaving the table. Within seconds of this young jerk's sitting at the table, he was talking to the dealer about the shift he was working on, for the casino!!! He didn't realize he was exposing himself as a shill! This was not the brightest or most typical of shills, but he messed things up, nonetheless. I left the casino.

Shills aside (and more important): I've made computer research discoveries that give you ample reason to avoid tables with awful players. (Old School researchers never covered this territory, and therefore were unaware of the very real factors that made bad players a threat to your winning potential.)

First, I've proven in my most recent computer studies that, *when players make intelligent moves, the dealer's*

Can Bad Players Mess Things Up At A Table?

busting rate actually goes up, therefore increasing your likelihood of winning. However, the reverse is also true -- bad players' moves will tend to lower the dealer's busting rate, therefore hurting your chances of winning.

Also -- and this is just as important a consideration -- my method to identify players' facedown cards at 1- and 2-deck tables (introduced in *Cutting Edge Blackjack*) works best when players are making predictable moves; bad players who make unpredictable moves make it impossible to predict what their facedown cards are. If they're being irrational, how can you predict the rationality of their moves? You can't.

Therefore, for all these many reasons, when you spot an extremely bad player, head for another table. They *will* hurt your chances of winning. I've *proven* that now, beyond a reasonable doubt.

Can You Make The Cards Better By Sitting Out A Round Or Adding A Betting Spot?

Can you change your fortune when the cards are bad by sitting out a round, or by going up and down in the number of betting spots you take? Some players seem to think so. But this approach is akin to performing voodoo; it will always come up empty. It's important that you understand why, so you know enough to avoid this fruitless desperation move in the future.

This tactic is based upon a lack of *knowledge*, which leads to a person acting on *hunches* and a vague idea that they can *influence* things somehow by doing *something*. Players who sit out a round or randomly change the number of betting spots they're playing often tell others at the table that they're doing it in order to shake things up. They might as well be reading tea leaves.

I'm not faulting the player; no blackjack books I am aware of have addressed this issue, and, until my most recent computer studies were completed, I don't believe a precise answer to this question was even available. Now that I've discovered numerous *repeating phenomena* through my

Can You Make The Cards Better?

research into card behavior, a player should no longer be in the dark about this issue.

First of all, there is something I've identified and named *orbiting associations.* This is a fancy term to describe the fact that large masses of cards repeat in the same round together, from shuffle to shuffle, because casino shuffling doesn't change the order of the cards very much.

In other words, if you looked at one round of action at a 7-player table, and you marked every card you saw with a red dot, you'd see about 70% or more of those cards being dealt *together* in the same round following the *next* shuffle!

Knowing this alone, you should now realize that the commonly used tactic of dropping out a round or adding a betting spot to change things for the better will, in general, not work. If the cards are bad, it's often due to *the composition of cards that are part of those larger forces*, the *orbiting associations*, which will not be so easily changed.

Second of all, a smart player learns how to do *card analysis* (using a system such as my Card Observation method in *Blackjack The SMART Way* or my more advanced Strategic Card Analysis method in *Cutting Edge Blackjack*), so they can detect when the cards are *bad* – and whether they're just bad in the player's *betting spot*, or if the whole *table* is bad. Then, upon recognizing card patterns that result in bad player hands, the smart player will *react* to what he or she sees.

I don't know if you've ever noticed this, but even at tables that most players would say are good (in other words, more than half are winning), there are usually some who are losing. It's rare when *everyone's* winning. The losers experience bad hands largely because of *betting spot repetition* – where many of the same cards are actually dealt to *the very same betting spot*, shuffle after shuffle! This is another repeating phenomenon first identified in *Cutting Edge Blackjack*, of which you should be aware.

New Ways To Win MORE At Blackjack

The solution to being at one of the losing spots at an overall *winning* table are: a) taking one or two *extra* betting spots (since the cards are good and most betting spots are winning, the probability is that you'd have at least one spot that's winning; but you'd have to make *smaller* bets in the *losing* spot to take advantage of this tactic); b) you can move to a different *seat*, in an attempt to *steal* someone's winning streak (sit to the right of that person); or c) if you're afraid of doing the previous two suggestions, *leave* the table.

Now, if you've analyzed the cards and found them to be very bad for *everyone* (you've identified a detrimental high-low-high-low card flow pattern, for example), then the only solution is to *leave* the table.

But, no matter what you do, it is never advisable to go in and out of the action or randomly change the number of hands you're playing, without reason, in a vain attempt at making the cards better. Those approaches don't work; plus, they'll lead to confusion and unwarranted losses.

Picking A Good Table: What Would YOU Have Done?

How good are you at picking a table?

Here's the scenario I faced the other day at a small casino:

There were three blackjack tables open.

One was a 1-deck game with four players. There, you could only double down on 9s, 10s and 11s and no doubling was allowed after splitting. As I watched the table a floor manager (dressed differently than the dealers) took over for the dealer, giving me a purposeful glance as she did so. These seats were open: the one next to the third baseman, the second baseman's seat, and the one next to the first baseman.

Then there was a 2-deck table with six players with just one betting spot open, next to the first baseman. There were only six chairs at the table and the players were huddled together as if they did not want anyone entering the game. A new dealer was brought in as I observed the action.

Also, there was another 2-deck table where all but one of the players had left during the time I'd been at the casino. As I approached that table, two new players sat down, and the pit boss rushed over and whispered something in the dealer's ear. These seats were open: the third baseman's seat and the one next to it; the second baseman's seat; and the one next to the first baseman.

Now, what would *you* have done in this situation? Where would you have sat?

Here's what I did: I *left*. Why?

The 1-deck table had *severe restrictions on doubling* (a penalty of at least 2% in my bottom line). Because of the *player arrangement*, I could not play more than one betting spot at a time (a valuable option). Most important was the red flag, *the floor manager taking over for the dealer (a highly unusual development)*. I felt it was an indication that I was getting too much scrutiny.

(A friend who was with me had remarked later: "Did you see how the pit bosses and floor mangers were watching you?" She had felt they had either identified me or that my appearance was attracting too much attention.)

Regarding the first 2-deck table, that was no good, either. Number one, *I never sit in or next to the first baseman's seat* (I wouldn't see enough cards before my turn in order to make an intelligent card move with any accuracy). Number two, *I'd have had to face an apparently hostile player environment*; I'd have had to push my way in (bringing a chair with me), against their wishes, and their hostility would have been a distraction. In pushing my way in *I also would have attracted way too much attention* (I always want to keep a low profile). Plus, *I wondered why a new dealer had been brought in* (looking at my watch, it didn't seem to the normal shift change time).

Picking A Good Table: What Would YOU Have Done?

About the second 2-deck table: *I suspected the cards were bad*, with all the players who had just left it. Also, *there were too few players at the table* (my computer studies having revealed that the higher the number of betting spots being played the higher your likelihood of winning). Plus, *I got the feeling the pit boss had whispered to the dealer: "If that guy sits down, I'm going to swap you out,"* meaning trouble lay ahead. Or, perhaps she discussed some other countermeasure with the dealer. That was my sixth sense talking, and my sixth sense is pretty good. *If you spot countermeasures in the making, the best response is often to leave the casino.*

So, I walked out *without ever playing*. I wonder how many readers have done that.

This is an option you ought to keep in your pocket. As the saying goes: discretion is the better part of valor.

Get A Huge Edge: Learn To Identify The Hole Card

Correct me if I'm wrong, but, if the issue of the dealer's hole card was given *any* attention in books that came before mine, their only advice was the glib suggestion that you should *"always assume the hole card is a 10."*

I'm sure you've heard that at some point. *Most* players who've come to my book events and seminars have heard that specious advice. In fact, it's one of the few phrases they can intone together, firmly etched in their collective memories. When I ask: "What did they tell you about the hole card? Always assume..." they inevitably chime in with: "...that the hole card is a 10!"

When I explain how flawed that advice is, jaws drop. Yet simple math proves how wrong that advice is:

After all, how many 10 point cards *are* there in a deck of cards? Sixteen, right? Do the math: 16/52 = 30.77%. So, if you assume the hole card to be a 10, you'll RIGHT about 31% of the time, and WRONG more than 69% of the time! That's not what I call playing the percentages correctly.

Get A Huge Edge: Learn To Identify The Hole Card

Yet, for DECADES, that's how many players dealt with the hole card problem, following advice that was absolutely wrong. Amazingly enough, someone actually tried to *defend* that faulty reasoning at one of my recent book signing events, saying, "There are a lot more 10s than any other card!" Yes, but the numbers above reflect a very different mathematical *probability* prognostication. I don't suppose that skeptic would be terribly happy if his boss told him: "Congratulations! You have a 31% likelihood of getting a raise this year!" You have to understand what the numbers are telling you. Thirty-one percent represents a minority situation.

There's another way of proving the old "assume the hole card is a 10" strategy is wacko:

The average score of the dealer's Ace is 19.57 if you include Blackjacks; if you don't, it's 18.83. *If the "assume the hole card is a 10" method was accurate, the Ace's average score would be 21!* But the truth is that it's much LESS!

The average score attained over time by the dealer's 7 is *18.01. That's a point HIGHER than it would be if the old advice were true.* Etc.

Clearly, you've got to chuck the old advice.

Knowing the likely identity of the hole card would give you a lot more power than previously thought possible. After all, if you knew what the dealer's first two cards were, you'd have a *very* good idea of whether the dealer would score or bust. Then, you could adjust your strategy accordingly, and play a more precise game.

For decades, the identity of the hole card remained a mystery. The designers of the first computer-produced blackjack strategies (and their followers, to this day) absolutely ignored the dealer's hole card, in spite of its crucial effect on the dealer's outcome. Perhaps they felt it was impossible to identify.

Undoubtedly this was because they used their computer's *random* number generator to *simulate* the data they later studied to produce their strategies. But blackjack *simulated* with a *random* number generator would have given them the false idea that you can't figure out what the hole card is because that's a *random* event. If they had used real cards in their research instead, they would have discovered otherwise, for cards do not play out randomly.

So, what *should* you do?

In a prior column you learned how *card imbalances* are like flashing lights to good card analysts. In fact, *imbalances reveal important clues regarding the hole card's identity.*

Imbalances *on the table* speak volumes about imbalances in the *undealt* cards. *If the undealt cards are rich in any type of card, their higher-than-normal proportions reflect a higher-than-normal likelihood of their being dealt.*

Now, understand that all we need is a high level of precision in predicting the hole card's identity to greatly increase our winning rate. We will NOT achieve 100% accuracy; that's unattainable. It'd be rare that *100%* of the undealt cards would either help or hurt the dealer.

But, we can ferret out what result the *majority* of those cards would produce, and, therefore, what the greatest *likelihood* is of any event occurring. The laws of mathematical probability would then tell us *it's smart to assume that the majority likelihood will occur, in choosing our card strategy.*

For example, in the second round of a 1-deck, 7-player practice game at one of my recent seminars, I predicted not only that the dealer's 5 would have a 9 or 10 in the hole, but that the dealer would most likely *bust*. How could I tell? Just one 9 had been dealt up to then, and the 10s were greatly underplayed in both rounds, so the undealt cards were rich in cards that would combine to bust the 5. The 5 busted! How powerful is that kind of skill?

After the round, we looked at the undealt cards. About 75% were 9s or 10s. Of course, if one of the 25% minority cards had been in the hole or had been dealt as the dealer's first hit card, the dealer might have scored. This illustrates that *you will sometimes lose in spite of making the right move*. However, *you need to play the percentages*, which means making decisions based upon the *highest likelihood* of something happening. So, in the example above, it was wise to assume the dealer would bust.

During the first round of another 7-player practice game, I knew in an instant that the hole card was most likely a 10. Why? Just three 10-point cards had been dealt. In a balanced situation, seven 10s would have been dealt by the end of the round. The imbalance indicated that 10s were overdue when the hole card was dealt. (And the hole card *was* indeed a 10.)

Every dealer up card has its strong and weak phases. What's the difference, after all, between a 10 sitting on a 6 in the hole, or a 6 sitting on a 10 in the hole?

The answer is: *no* difference! ...Except you've been taught *always to fear the 10, and always pull to a 17 against it*, which – when the 10 is weak – is a *faulty* strategy.

With hole card prediction skills, you'll never again be playing in the dark.

Let's look, for instance, at the first-round card example at the top of the next page (it doesn't matter how many decks are in play – the principle involved remains the same for all blackjack games, although your accuracy level will be greater the fewer the decks involved). Uncovering the hole card's likely identity in this example makes a huge difference in knowing how to play the third baseman's hand of 12 points.

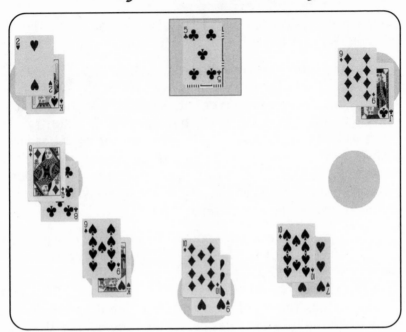

A Basic Strategist would say: "Always stand on 12s versus the dealer's 5!" But, in this case, the dealer's too strong to do that. How do we know that?

Because mathematical probability tells you that the hole card is unlikely to be a 7, 8, 9 or 10 (the cards that combine with the 5 to give the 5 its most bustable two-card scores – 12, 13, 14 and 15, respectively).

How do we know this?

If the cards were balanced, with 13 cards on the table, we should see one of each type of card. But we don't. There's an imbalance heavy in high cards.

The 7s through 10s have already been dealt in average or above-average proportions. The 9s are over-represented (there should be one at most); so are the 10s (at a 6-player table there should only be four 10s among the first two cards dealt, as I explain in *Cutting Edge Blackjack*). Plus, only one low card has been dealt – the 2. This imbalance tells us that low cards and Aces are in higher proportion than normal among the cards we don't know (the hole card and the undealt cards). So, there's a higher-than-normal probability that the hole card will be a low card or an Ace – the best cards in helping the dealer's 5 attain a good score and not bust – and so the dealer has a high likelihood of attaining a good score.

What's more, I've proven that when it's unlikely there's an 8, 9 or 10 in the hole, the dealer's 5 has a paltry 24% probability of busting (almost half what you've been told to expect) – and so it plays out more like the dealer's 8. Therefore, in the example above, you would *play* the dealer's 5 like an 8, and *hit* your 12.

That demonstrates the power you acquire, the precision, when you know how to figure out what's in the hole, with a great deal of accuracy.

So – to summarize - one key to identifying the hole card is identifying the *imbalances* among the cards dealt since the last shuffle. Those that were over-played are less likely to be in the hole. Those that were under-played (or not dealt at all) are that much more likely to be in the hole.

And this is only scratching the surface of the power you will wield once you achieve more and more precision in ferreting out the identity of the hole card.

Learning this skill is one of the keys to pushing the winning envelope in blackjack. And you can take that to the bank.

...More on this topic in my column on Ducks & Bucks.

Introducing...
The Weakened Ace

Correct me if I'm wrong, but, whenever I read about how strong the dealer's Ace is, the writer says the Ace's busting rate is in the 10 to 11% range. In other words, they're including the times that the Ace combines with the hole card to give the dealer a blackjack.

The only problem is...when the dealer has a blackjack...YOU have NO TURN! Therefore, including blackjacks in these statistics is meaningless, if you want to devise a proper strategy against the Ace.

The point I'm making is twofold: any strategies based upon dealer busting numbers that include the blackjacks are faulty; and to understand what you're up against, you need different numbers, the ones that pertain to the Ace when it does NOT achieve a blackjack. Once you have the correct numbers, you'll see that the dealer's Ace has some exploitable weaknesses.

What I'm doing here is introducing you to what I call the **Weakened Ace**. The Weakened Ace (which I represent by the symbol A^w) is my term for the dealer's Ace *as you face*

Introducing...The Weakened Ace

it. Without a 10 in the hole, it combines with weaker cards to achieve overall weaker results than you've been led to believe.

Its vulnerability is best expressed in its *score profile*. A score profile is my term for a breakdown of how often a dealer's up card achieves each of the five winning scores (17, 18, 19, 20 and 21) or *busts*. So, let's look at these figures:

Unlike what you've probably read in other books and articles, *the true busting rate of the Ace you face, the Weakened Ace, is just over 15%* — nearly 50% higher than the figures promulgated by Old School writers.

In addition, it achieves an average score of just 18.83 (nearly one point lower than the Ace overall, whose average is 19.57). **In this aspect, it ranks SEVENTH among the ten dealer up cards.**

Do you know what average score *you* achieve, over time, when you pull to a 17 or better? Not 18, as some would say, but *19 (which is higher than the A^w's average score)*. Get the idea?

It draws to a 19 or better less than 50% of the time (45%, to be exact)! **Furthermore, the Weakened Ace ranks SIXTH when it comes to the percent of times it achieves the best winning score, 21 (6.74%).**

Don't get me wrong – the Weakened Ace is not a *weak* up card, overall. What I'm pointing out are its Achilles heels.

How To Exploit The A^w

Given what I've told you above, you should realize that I've just given you some additional profitable opportunities; you can make more money off the dealer's Ace than you previously thought.

For instance, if you've drawn a hard total of 11 and you know that you are very likely to draw an 8, 9 or 10 with the next hit card (because, in analyzing the cards that have been dealt to this point, you noticed that 8s, 9s and 10s were greatly under-represented), this would be a good time to *double* (a move that's *not* wise if you are not aware of the A^w 's weaknesses, and cannot identify this particular card imbalance).

Another example: if you're holding a 9 or 10 and card analysis tells you that the undealt cards are rich in Aces and 10s (let's say it's the second round of a 1-deck, 7-player game, and, up to now, you've seen NO Aces and four or less 10s were dealt), that's also a great time to double down. Remember -- the Weakened Ace draws to an average score of less than 19.

If you're a beginner and you haven't yet learned my card analysis methods, you might find that my All-Inclusive Card Counting System (introduced in *Blackjack The SMART Way*) will provide you with a good entry-level way of a way to discover when you can exploit the dealer's Weakened Ace.

In my All-Inclusive Card Counting System, you keep track of ALL the cards, so it's more accurate than counting systems that don't. You count the 2s through 7s as +1 point apiece, as they're dealt, and 8s through 10-point cards as – 1 point apiece (we keep track of the number of Aces separately). So, if you've seen three 2s, one 3, one 6 and four 10s, for example, the count would be +1, pointing out a slight imbalance in favor of the low cards. The higher the number – either in a positive or negative direction – the more likely it is that cards on the other end of the spectrum will be coming with the next cards dealt. Get a high positive number, and high cards (as I defined them above) are overdue. And vice versa.

So, for example, if you're at a 6-deck table and you've drawn a hard total of 11 versus the dealer's Ace, and the All-Inclusive count was rather neutral or negative when the dealer's hole card was dealt but is +8 or greater when your

Introducing...The Weakened Ace

turn arrives (revealing an imbalance in which 8s, 9s and 10s are overdue), this would be a good time to *double down* on your hand of 11 points because of the A^w 's relative weakness in achieving scores of 19 or better.

The Weakened 10

Now (as you might have already surmised), there is such a thing as a Weakened 10, too. That's the dealer 10 you face, which does not have an Ace in the hole for a Blackjack. But, unfortunately, *the Weakened 10 (which we will represent by the symbol 10^w) is better for the dealer in many respects than the Weakened Ace!*

The Weakened 10 has a higher average score than the Weakened Ace (19.09). The 10^w also does much better in the 20+ category -- *the 10^w attains the highest winning scores (20 and 21) nearly one and a half times as often as the A^w!* The 10^w also outperforms the A^w in the 19+ category. Plus, it scores totals of 20 nearly *twice* as often as the A^w!

Beginners will have trouble identifying the situations in which they might exploit the dealer's Weakened 10. The one obvious Achilles heel it has is also to be found in its score profile. *The 10^w achieves scores of 21 only 4% of the time! That's the lowest average of all the up cards!*

Once you've developed good card analysis skills, you will therefore recognize new situations where you should put more money on the table -- when you are likely to achieve the top winning score, a 21, knowing that the dealer's 10^w has a 96% chance of not even pushing with you and a 0% chance of beating you. That's when you have a hand of 11 points and 10s are way overdue when your turn arrives.

This gives you something to ponder. Because these are numbers you can take to the bank.

The Truth About The Up Cards -- · Part One

At my book signing events, one question I always ask is: "How many of the dealer's up cards bust more than 50% of the time?" It is rare that I get the correct answer.

Many don't have a clue. Others shout out with confidence and pride: "The 5 and 6 do!" Some usually then add: "And the 4!"

The correct answer is: *none*. Unfortunately, even the few who know the answer to this question rarely know much more about the up cards. I've never met anyone who knew their particulars, such as their winning rates, rankings, score profiles, or average scores.

Players are not necessarily to blame for this. This information (detailed in the "What's Your Up Card IQ?" chapter of *Cutting Edge Blackjack*) is not, to my knowledge, readily available outside of my books. (See the chart at the end of this column and study it to really get to know the up cards!)

Yet, all of this is a crucial part of a player's understanding of how to play the game. You cannot adopt a flexible, highly

The Truth About The Up Cards -- Part One

accurate card strategy, or maximize your winning rate, without this knowledge; without it, you're playing in the dark and are undoubtedly frustrated.

...Like the player who told me how upset he was with his lack of success using Old School methods: "I stand on my stiffs (12s through 16s) against the dealer's 4, but the dealer usually beats me with 20s and 21s!"

"Well, yes," I replied. "That's understandable – the 4 causes the dealer to bust 43% of the time, so, conversely, the dealer will *beat* your stiffs *57% of the time!*"

In fact, the 4 draws to the second highest average score – 19.01 – just behind the 19.09 attained by the dealer's Weakened 10!* Plus, the 4 gives the dealer the top winning scores of 21 and 20 points 24.39% of the time – ranking FOURTH behind the dealer's 10, Ace and 2!

The point is, you should especially get to know each up card's *score profile* (my term for their score performance, over time). Now that you know that no up card busts a majority of times, you should appreciate why this is so important. After all, if up cards *score* more than they *bust*, their score profiles show you what you're really up against – they detail the up cards' strengths and weaknesses.

Score profiles are unique to each up card. Cards are just numbers, and they combine with the others differently. Because of this, each up card achieves the five winning scores (17, 18, 19, 20 and 21) *different percentages of times*.

For instance, let's look at some telling aspects of the score profile of the dealer's 7:

It causes the dealer to achieve a score of 17 (the *lowest*

---

* The Weakened 10 – a concept I introduced to you in a another column - is the dealer's 10 in a non-Blackjack situation; the 10 you actually play against.

winning score) *nearly 41% of the time!* It achieves an 18 (the second-lowest winning score) 12% of the time. And it makes the dealer bust almost 26% over time.

Do you realize what those numbers are telling you? They say that *the dealer's 7 either busts or reaches the two below-average winning scores more than 78% of the time!* So, you'll *beat* it more than not because a player's average winning score is 19 (in spite of what you might have read to the contrary)! Therein lies the weakness of the dealer's 7!

To top this off, the dealer's average score with the 7 is *the lowest of any up card:* 18.01! In addition (and you won't learn this from anyone else), *when there's unlikely to be a 10 or Ace in the hole, the dealer's 7 busts 42% of the time!* In those situations, therefore, you should play it like it's a 4, 5, or 6! The opportunities for higher gains with creative card moves, given this information, are endless. Herein lies the weakness of the 7. (My books were the first to reveal this fact; most writers still seem unaware of it.)

By the way, score profiles also tell you how YOUR cards will perform in a splitting situation, if you draw to a 17. For example – referring back to the above — split two 7s, and now you know that you'll achieve a score of 17 about 41% over time, your bust rate will be 26%, etc.!

These are numbers you should know. Otherwise, you'll be a slave to someone's Basic Strategy approach, which, as a cookie-cutter approach to a complex problem, will typically only give you break-even win/loss results -- at *best*.

As an Intermediate or Advanced player, when you have the skills to determine when the dealer is *unlikely* to bust, this kind of score information will be powerful stuff in choosing your best card move. We'll look at that issue in the column on Ducks & Bucks.

Meanwhile, study the chart on the next page. *Really* get to know the up cards' unique strengths and weaknesses.

The Truth About The Up Cards -- Part One

UP CARD VITAL STATISTICS SUMMARY

(Reproduced from *Cutting Edge Blackjack* © 2004 Richard Harvey)

UP CARD	BUST %	AVG SCORE	%BJs	%21s	%20s	%19s	%18s	%17s
2	35.42	18.97	N/A	12.17	12.89	13.49	12.65	13.37
3	37.76	18.94	N/A	11.27	12.85	10.65	15.58	11.88
4	43.12	19.01	N/A	12.01	12.38	9.96	10.05	12.47
5	42.47	18.94	N/A	11.04	11.76	10.67	12.12	11.94
6	41.96	18.80	N/A	10.81	9.91	10.00	11.99	15.32
7	25.75	18.01	N/A	5.97	8.12	7.46	12.13	40.58
8	23.91	18.53	N/A	7.61	8.15	12.91	36.01	11.41
9	23.00	18.86	N/A	6.48	10.61	38.03	9.39	12.49
10	20.38	19.30	7.94	3.65	35.42	11.59	10.35	10.68
10^w	22.14	19.09	N/A	3.96	38.47	12.59	11.24	11.60
Ace	10.28	19.57	31.02	4.77	14.05	12.88	12.63	14.38
A^w	15.04	18.83	N/A	6.74	19.61	18.65	18.29	21.54

The Truth About The Up Cards -- Part Two

Just as Einstein gave physics its $E=mc^2$ defining equation, blackjack's computer researchers of the early 1960s suggested they had discovered blackjack's defining equation — the one that led to the concept of Basic Strategy.

For Einstein's equation to hold true, c, the speed of light, must be a *constant*. In other words, its *value* must *always* be the *same*. And, indeed, Einstein was able to *prove* that, no matter whether emitted from a moving or a stationery source, the speed of light is always 186,000 miles per second.

Similarly, for blackjack's defining equation to hold true, the number representing the dealer up cards' behavior over time (their *busting rates* and *score profiles*, for example) must be *constants* for it to produce *one* recommended move per up card *per player total*.

Unfortunately, blackjack's defining equation does not hold up to scrutiny. *Its "constants" are not true constants.*

The Truth About The Up Cards -- Part Two

And here's the faulty equation blackjack's computer research pioneers used to develop Basic Strategy:

(DB-(DB*PB)) - P17*D18 - P17*D19 - P17*D20 - P17*D21 - P17*DBJ + P18*D17 - P18*D19 - P18*D20 - P18*21 - P18*DBJ + P19*D17 + P19*D18 - P19*D20 - P19*D21 - P19*DBJ + P20*D17 + P20*D18 + P20*D19 - P20*D21 - P20*DBJ + P21*D17 + P21*D18 + P21*D19 + P21*D20 - P21*DBJ = *the projected percentage of player wins or losses starting off with a specific 2-card hand vs. one of the up cards, when the player makes a particular move*

(Asterisks represent multiplication.)

To explain the algebraic terms:

DB represents the dealer up card's busting rate (an overall average determined after millions of computer-simulated blackjack rounds by the pioneer researchers). PB stands for the player's predicted busting rate when the player makes a particular move being tested. P17, P18, etc., represent the percentage of times the player was projected to achieve the score next to the P based upon the move chosen. D17, D18, etc., represent the percentage of times the dealer is projected to reach the score next to the D, based upon the up card and the way that card combines with the various hole cards and hit cards over millions of simulated blackjack rounds. DBJ is the percentage of times the dealer is projected to get a Blackjack.

P17*D18 will therefore give us the percentage of times the player will reach a score of 17 when starting off with a particular 2-card hand when the dealer is projected to attain a score of 18.

The algebraic figures (P17*D18, P20*D19, etc.) are *added* when the player's score is *higher* than the dealer's (showing, in theory, how often the player score would *beat* the dealer score designated). Conversely, the figures are *subtracted* when the *dealer* score is higher than the player score (theoretically showing how often the dealer score would beat the player score). For instance, P17*D19 is subtracted because this represents a projected player *loss* (theoretically showing how often the player will draw to a 17 when the dealer draws a total of 19).

(Note that player gains from dealer busting are adjusted for the percentage of times the player will bust at the same time, resulting in a player loss; this is represented by the algebraic figure DB*PB.)

Now, for the equation on the prior page to be valid, the dealer up card numbers (busting rates and score percentages) must be constants. This is where the fathers of the late 20th Century methods went wrong. My most recent computer studies have revealed that these numbers are anything BUT constant. They, in fact, vary dramatically over time!

The whole premise of the Old School approach falls apart if the numbers that need to be plugged into its defining equation are constantly changing. Therefore, *since blackjack's defining equation of the late 20th Century makes no sense, the methods that resulted were based upon bad math and are deeply flawed.*

In other words, if the dealer's 2 *doesn't* dependably bust 35% of the time as blackjack's Old School researchers predicted, then their using 35% as a constant (as "DB" in the equation) produced *faulty* recommendations for playing against the dealer's 2 — and so on, for each up card.

In the next column: more startling truths about the up cards.

The Truth About The Up Cards -- Part Three

What if I told you there were ten different alien aircraft the Air Force had been tracking, each characterized by different colors, each displaying the ability to travel at three different speeds unique to each color. If you wanted to shoot them down, how would you go about it?

For instance, if the blue craft's three speeds were 1000, 2000 and 7000 m.p.h., would you fire an antiaircraft missile going 5000 m.p.h., the average of the three speeds? What hope of success would you have doing that? (None.)

If you're laughing, then I hope you're not a Basic Strategy player. Because this is *exactly* the approach taken by blackjack's 20th Century strategists in devising that strategy. They summed up the results of 8 million or more rounds of simulated blackjack action, and then made strategy recommendations based upon the average busting rate (and score profile) of each up card over that period of time. (Instead of aircraft speeds as in the example above, they threw many wildly different types of blackjack situations together in coming up with their averages.)

New Ways To Win MORE At Blackjack

The fact that this approach produced fractional advantages with 1-deck games and losing results for games with more decks (by their own admission) is no surprise.

As I have discovered in my most recent computer studies, *you cannot count on the dealer's 2 busting 35% of the time, or the 3 busting 38% of the time, etc., as you've undoubtedly been taught.* If you and I went to a casino and charted the results at any table, over any amount of time that day, *it would be rare for any ONE of the up cards to bust at the rate the researchers of old had predicted.*

The chart on the next page (a tiny slice of results from my latest computer studies) shows you how up cards *actually behave. They display a range of variable busting rates when analyzed in chunks of time more accurately reflecting players' average playing sessions.*

The percentages in each box of the chart reflect periods covering 25 appearances of the up card specified, equivalent to roughly 5.5 hours of playing time at the casino. (Of course, the *exact* time it takes before you've seen 25 of each up card varies, depending upon the speed of the dealer, the number of players at the table, the speed of the players, and so on). Each successive box, going down, shows you the busting rate chalked up in the next 5.5 hour period (often, with a different set of cards). The grey boxes on the bottom show you the overall range of busting rates a player would have experienced had they played during all 10 of these 5.5-hour periods. (Note: the range would have been even *greater* had we analyzed shorter time periods.)

One thing this chart shows you is that, on any given day, the dealer's 4 could bust a paltry 32% of the time; or it might bust at an amazingly generous rate of 60% (a higher rate than the Old School said any card should bust)! The dealer's 10 might exhibit a pretty good busting rate of 36%, nearly twice what the Old School books tell you it should be, or, a measly 4%, which is far less than the Old

The Truth About The Up Cards -- Part Three

2	3	4	5	6	7	8	9	10	A
48%	40%	32%	52%	56%	20%	16%	24%	8%	12%
28%	24%	36%	44%	24%	16%	12%	32%	4%	16%
40%	48%	40%	44%	32%	28%	20%	8%	8%	8%
28%	44%	48%	44%	44%	32%	0%	36%	20%	12%
40%	48%	52%	48%	40%	20%	20%	20%	24%	28%
24%	36%	40%	52%	32%	16%	40%	16%	36%	16%
32%	40%	40%	40%	24%	28%	20%	28%	16%	8%
48%	36%	60%	28%	32%	20%	20%	20%	12%	16%
16%	36%	32%	48%	36%	36%	32%	40%	32%	16%
28%	52%	40%	28%	36%	44%	52%	16%	24%	24%
16-48%	24-52%	32-60%	28-52%	24-56%	16-44%	0-52%	8-40%	4-36%	8-28%

Schoolers predicted even the Ace would bust.

This is your reality – one that you must learn to deal with if you want to make card moves with any kind of precision. Fortunes are often made or lost in the course of a day, or several days. You cannot wait for 8 million rounds to go by (a practical impossibility, by the way) to turn a profit.

In Part Four: a way to profit from this discovery.

The Truth About The Up Cards -- Part Four

There's an adage they teach in college statistics courses: *Figures lie and liars figure.* Statistics can, unfortunately, be used to deceive, and they often are. Additionally, there are cases where statistics are simply misused. Researchers are sometimes misled by invalid applications of math in solving a problem. *This is exactly what happened with blackjack's earliest computer-reliant researchers.* Summing together wildly different blackjack situations, they then used the *average* dealer busting rate from those disparate card situations to come up with Basic Strategy and other faulty methods. This global approach to arriving at card move decisions (which instead should be dealt with by analyzing the specific reality players face in any particular round) produced break-even results at best. Their followers in the years since have used their dubious statistics to con players into thinking theirs was the "Way" -- and the *only* way.

Yet, in my last column, you saw how wrong they were in concluding that dealer up card busting rates are predictably constant. So, how do you deal with this troubling reality?

The Truth About The Up Cards -- Part Four

One solution I devised involved taking my computer research data for each up card and subtracting situations by hole card type to see the effect it produced on the dealer's busting rate. This was a valid way of using statistics, and very telling. Doing things in this way lets us know how we must adjust our strategy to the reality at hand, each round, based on our analysis of the card imbalances on the table.

After all, if we know the dealer's likely busting rate, and it's far different than predicted by the inventors of Basic Strategy, then we'd be crazy not to adopt a more precise strategy – making a card move befitting the probable busting rate of the moment. (Each up card has its weak and strong phases, based upon what's in the hole.)

Look at the first-round card situation below, for example. How would you play the third baseman's hand of 12 points?

An Old School Basic Strategist would say: "Always stand on 12s versus the dealer's 5!" But, in this case, if we apply more modern methods, we can see that the dealer's 5 is

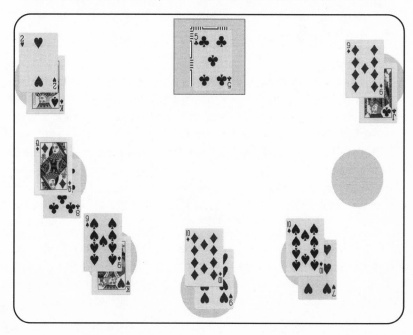

too strong to do that.

I say this because *the hole card is unlikely to be a 7, 8, 9 or 10* — those cards have already been dealt in average or above-average proportion. The 9s are over-represented (there should be one at most). So are the 10s — at a 6-player table there should only be four 10s among the first two cards dealt. (Follow my logic on the 10s: at a 6-player table, there are 14 cards initially dealt, 13 of which are more or less known, if you use my method of identifying facedown cards at 1- and 2-deck tables. There are four 10-point cards for every 13 cards in the deck, so that's how many you should see after the first two cards are dealt at a 6-player table.)

And my computer research has shown that *when it's unlikely there's an 8, 9 or 10 in the hole, the dealer's 5 has a paltry 24% probability of busting* (almost half what you've been told to expect) — more akin to the dealer's 8. Therefore, you should *play* it like an 8, and *hit* your 12. (The 8s, 9s and 10s in the hole give the dealer the most bustable two-card scores with a 5: 13, 14 and 15. Without those, the dealer is much more likely to attain a good score.)

In sum: *your job as a 21st Century player is to use the information revealed in my computer studies to determine whether the dealer's up card is in a strong or weak phase* (based upon the cards that have been dealt), *and react to it accordingly.* In this way, you'll play with greater precision based upon the facts at hand, instead using the imprecise Old School methods that are based upon a prediction of how the up card (without respect to its differing behavior over time) would play out *over the course of 10 player lifetimes.*

In the next column, I'll help you make more accurate card moves by introducing you to my Ducks & Bucks method of identifying when each up card is especially strong or weak.

The Ducks & Bucks Method: Is The Up Card Weak or Strong?

On numerous occasions I've offered to make a wager with any of the Old School writers but none of them has taken me up on this offer. Here's what I've suggested: We'd watch the action at a blackjack table for a number of hours, representing a typical playing session of the average blackjack player. (A stenographer would record the results.) Then we'd calculate the busting rate of each of the dealer up cards during that period. I'd pay the Old Schooler a set amount (determined in advance) for each up card that busted at the "constant" rate the Old Schooler's books say it should; they'd pay me for each up card that *didn't*.

I'll tell you why no one's taken me up on this offer: they know that I'd come away a big winner every time. And if they KNOW I'd win this little wager, it's because they *know* their methods are faulty. The lynchpin of the methods first introduced in the 1960s was that each dealer up card busted at a *predictable, constant* rate. (The 2 was supposed to bust at a constant rate of 35%, the 3, 38%, etc.) *Without that, those methods – still being used by many players today - have no validity.*

Yet, in prior columns, you have seen how the up cards *really* behave. Their busting rates fluctuate *wildly*. It'd be rare for even *one* of the ten different dealer up cards to bust as often as the Old School writers say it will, in any given playing period. Do you realize what that fact is telling you? If you're using Old School methods, based upon mistaken notions about dealer busting rates, *you're going to make wrong card moves most of the time!*

The good thing is that I was able to devise new playing methods that take this reality into account, so you can play with greater precision -- my Ducks & Bucks method (introduced in *Cutting Edge Blackjack*) works great in this way. Every one of the dealer's up cards has weak and strong phases. When an up card is especially weak (when the dealer is likely to lose to more players than would be considered normal for that up card), I call it a *Duck* (which is an acronym for *Diminished Up Card*). A Duck will bust much *more* than the Old School predicted it would. In rounds where an up card is especially strong (when the dealer is likely to beat many more players, over time, than would be considered normal for that up card), I call that up card a Buck (which is an acronym for *Brutal Up Card*. A Buck will bust much *less* than the Old School predicted it would.

Each particular mix of cards (as determined by the initial shuffling of new cards) produces its own peculiar set of up card busting rates. What we're most concerned with, though, is learning to accurately predict the results of any one particular round. *That largely depends upon what is most likely to be in the hole*. In assessing what's likely to be the hole card, we also want to know the reverse -- what's NOT likely to be in the hole. *This* will tell us whether an up card is a Duck or Buck (or neither).

In a prior column, you learned a good deal about my method for identifying the dealer's hole card. In this column, let's use that skill, along with other card analysis skills

The Ducks & Bucks Method

we've discussed, to show you how you might ferret out situations where the up card is a Duck, and then use that power to alter your strategy to your financial benefit.

For instance, let's look at the dealer's 7. When might that be a Duck? If you're playing a 1-deck game, and all four Aces were dealt in the first round, and the 10s have all but been played out by your turn in the second round, that 7 is likely a Duck. Why? *When the dealer's 7 is not sitting on an Ace or 10, the dealer's overall busting rate is 42%! That's roughly how often the dealer's 4-6 bust, overall.* So, *you should play the 7 Duck like you would play the dealer's 4-6* (according to my Basic Strategy directions for those up cards -- see that on page 79)! Instead of *hitting* your Ace-2 through Ace-6 vs. the 7 Duck, *you should double down.* Instead of *standing* on an Ace-7, you should *double.* Instead of *standing* on your pair of 9s, you should *split.*

Here are a few more examples of Ducks you should get to know:

When it's unlikely the dealer's 8 has a 10 in the hole, its overall busting rate is 32%. When the dealer's 9 is not likely sitting on a 10, its overall busting rate is 34%. Those elevated busting rates are more akin to the dealer's 2, and so you should play those Ducks like you play the dealer's 2 (using my Basic Strategy formula). You should *split* your pairs of 2s and 7s instead of hitting them; and *you should stand on your hands of 13 points or higher!* With the 9, you should *double* on your 10 point hands instead of hitting.

Of course, making these unorthodox moves will puzzle the dealer and your fellow players. That's OK. It's your money. (These types of unusual moves will not red flag you.) If neighboring players grumble, play dumb. (You don't want the house to know you're a player using any kind of system; they'll throw countermeasures at you, or even bar you, if you get good enough.) If the casino thinks you're stupid, so much the better -- they'll leave you alone. If players scratch their heads with your moves (when you're actually *smarter* than they are, and *winning* more), who cares? You will be laughing all the way to the bank.

On page 80, you will find two charts that will help you identify some of the easier-to-spot Ducks and Bucks. Now, I've identified three or four different types of Ducks and Bucks for each up card, but to show you them all here might be too overwhelming for all but the advanced players. Instead, these charts will give you just one Duck and Buck per up card -- the most useful ones, the ones that are easiest to spot. This will provide you with a good entry-level way to benefit from what my research has turned up, without pressuring you to learn everything all at once.

To identify when each up card fits the definition of one of the Ducks or Bucks listed on the charts, use the hole card identification skills I taught you in a prior column. With these charts, you'll be kind of looking in *reverse*: you'll be searching for a Duck or Buck based upon what cards are NOT likely to be in the hole (the dealer's facedown card). Start by trying to memorize and spot the Ducks and Bucks for just a few of the up cards. Choose the ones that you think you can most easily remember at the casino. Then, over time, try to add more and more, until you're able to spot at least one type of Duck and Buck for each up card. With each additional Duck and Buck in your repertoire you'll be making more and more money, because you'll be playing a much more precise game. Practice this at home first -- with cards, and the charts on pages 79 and 80. Play out many, many rounds, looking for Ducks ands Bucks, until you're able to spot them quickly.

Now, there are rounds where the up cards are neither Ducks nor Bucks (the cards might be "neutral" or nearly balanced; or perhaps they're imbalanced in a way that doesn't clearly point to them being either a Duck or Buck). In those cases, you'd use my Basic Strategy (on the next page) if you're a beginner, or my card analysis methods if you're more skilled, to determine what your best moves

The Ducks & Bucks Method

should be. Your choice of moves would hinge mostly on what your hit cards are likely to be and your understanding of the relative strengths and weaknesses of the specific up card you're facing, based upon what you figured the hole card would be.

Have fun!* (H = hit; S = stand; D = double; Sp = split; SUR/H = surrender if allowed -- if not, hit.)

	2	3	4	5	6	7	8	9	10	A
4-8	H	H	H	H	H	H	H	H	H	H
9	H	D	D	D	D	D	H	H	H	H
10	D	D	D	D	D	D	D	H	H	H
11	D	D	D	D	D	D	D	D	H	H
12	H	H	S	S	S	H	H	H	H	H
13	S	S	S	S	S	H	H	H	H	H
14	S	S	S	S	S	H	H	H	H	Sur/H
15	S	S	S	S	S	H	H	H	Sur/H	Sur/H
16	S	S	S	S	S	H	H	Sur/H	Sur/H	Sur/H
17+	S	S	S	S	S	S	S	S	S	S
BJ	S	S	S	S	S	S	S	S	S	S
2,2	Sp	Sp	Sp	Sp	Sp	Sp	H	H	H	H
3,3	H	Sp	Sp	Sp	Sp	Sp	H	H	H	H
4,4	H	H	H	H	H	H	H	H	H	H
5,5	D	D	D	D	D	D	D	H	H	H
6,6	H	Sp	Sp	Sp	Sp	H	H	H	H	H
7,7	Sp	Sp	Sp	Sp	Sp	Sp	H	H	H	H
8,8	Sp	Sp	Sp	Sp	Sp	Sp	Sp	Sp	Sp	Sp
9,9	Sp	Sp	Sp	Sp	Sp	S	Sp	Sp	S	S
10,10	S	S	S	S	S	S	S	S	S	S
A,A	Sp	Sp	Sp	Sp	Sp	Sp	Sp	Sp	Sp	Sp
A2-A5	H	H	D	D	D	H	H	H	H	H
A6	H	D	D	D	D	H	H	H	H	H
A7	S	D	D	D	D	S	S	H	H	S
A8	S	S	S	S	S	S	S	S	S	S
A9	S	S	S	S	S	S	S	S	S	S
BJ	S	S	S	S	S	S	S	S	S	S

*Laminated, color versions of the charts on this and the next page (suitable for taking with you to the casino) are available. Simply send $7 for each set of charts you want (each set includes one Basic Strategy chart and one Ducks & Bucks chart) along with your name and address to: Mystic Ridge Books, P.O. Box 66930, Albuquerque, NM 87193.

Upcard	Not In Hole	Bust Rate	Play It Like
2	6s-9s	41%	4-6
3	7s&8s	41%	4-6
4	5s-7s	47%	Weak 4-6
5	3s-6s	48%	Weak 4-6
6	4s&5s	48%	Weak 4-6
7	10s	38%	3
7b	10s&As	42%	4-6
8	10s	32%	2
9	10s	34%	2
9b	8s&10s or 9s-As	40% or 43%	4-6
10	9s&10s	36%	2
10b	8s-10s	43%	4-6
Ace	6s-9s	33%	2

Upcard	Not In Hole	Bust Rate	Play It Like
2	10s	28%	Weak 7*
3	9s&10s	28%	Weak 7*
4	10s	35%	2
5	9s&10s	27%	Weak 7*
6	10s	28%	Weak 7*
6b	8s-10s	20%	10
7	9s	22%	10
7b	5s&6s	19%	10
8	8s	19%	10
8b	4s-6s	13%	Ace
9	7s	18%	10
9b	5s-7s	12%	Ace
10	5s&6s	14%	Weakened Ace
10b	4s-6s	10%	Ace
Ace	ANY 3 of 2s-5s	6%	Surrender 4s-7s & 12s-17s. No splits.

Weak 7 = Stand on 15s and above
ALL charts © 2004 by Richard Harvey

Your Powers of Observation
&
Keeping Track of Things

Most blackjack players I've met are of at least average if not above-average intelligence. And it doesn't take a mathematical genius to keep track of some of the more important factors that go into a smart, modern game strategy.

I've discovered through years of research that we can break down winning strategy into simple components that the average player can easily understand, in order to play a much better game.

The most important thing you need to do is *sharpen your powers of observation*. Look closely at what's been dealt, to detect any patterns - good or bad - that might affect your game.

In my books and seminars, I teach players an easy but systematic approach to card analysis; but even before you learn the ins and outs of this crucial skill, you can improve your game simply by paying attention to what's before you.

After all, that's the necessary first step in doing card analysis.

One Thing To Watch: The Cards After The First Shuffle

One thing to which you need to pay attention is how the cards play out immediately after new cards are brought in and are first shuffled.

I've proven in my computer research that shuffling does not change the order of the cards significantly. That tells you an awful lot.

For example, here's what you should do if, in paying attention to what's unfolding before you, you notice that the first shuffle produces a bad pattern of cards in which round after round goes rather poorly. *You should get up and find a better table. The cards are unlikely to be much better after the next shuffle.*

Furthermore, a bad shuffling job will most often produce a bad flow of cards. You can anticipate this by watching to see if the dealer is shuffling the cards in a standard fashion, or is giving it short shrift. *If the dealer's giving it the once over, you should get up and move to a different table even before he or she deals the first round from that poorly shuffled bunch.*

Now, if you don't know yet what to look for in dealer shuffling, *you can detect a bad shuffling job simply by observing how the cards come out.*

On a recent trip to Vegas, for instance, an inexperienced dealer did such a poor job of shuffling that - in every round - I noticed that most if not all of one suit was dealt (usually in sequential order) as well as most of the cards of a second suit in every round!

If you had trained yourself in the art of observation, it would have been hard NOT to pick up on this obvious and detrimental pattern. Yet *no one noticed this but myself!*

Your Powers of Observation/Keeping Track of Things

I left the table; everyone else stayed! This type of card pattern is *deadly* for your game.

At Least Keep Track of the Aces!

Now, beginners and intermediates are not going to be able to keep track of everything advanced players or pros do. But even beginners can keep track of how many *Aces* have been played. This is perhaps the most crucial card that affects your future fortune.

Use your fingers, use your chips – there are many simple ways of counting off the Aces - but *whatever you do, count those Aces!*

Here's just one tip you need remember with regard to Aces: *if all have been dealt, raise your bets to a higher level, perhaps three times your normal level, because the dealer is then much less likely to beat you!* (I'll give you more details on this phenomenon in two later columns.)

Although that advice contradicts much of what you've probably been taught, that's one thing I've proven in my most recent computer studies.

Other Cards To Especially Watch

Conversely, if you notice that all the 9s have been dealt (and, to a lesser extent, the 7s and 8s), all things being equal (in other words, the rest of the cards being roughly balanced), you should lower your bet to your minimum bet level. You are now likely to experience double-digit losses.

The main thing to remember is that your most important tools are your eyes...and everyone has them!

In the next column, we'll look at how you can spot card imbalances, and how that skill can make you a bigger winner.

With Card Analysis: First Identify The Imbalances

Imbalances rule the game of blackjack. They're the key to uncovering the mathematical probability of any event occurring (the likelihood of your getting the hit card you need, for instance). They determine what your card strategy should be.

To identify imbalances, you need to know that the cards are considered *balanced* when each card is in the same proportion they were in the box (where non-10s each account for 7.69% of the mix, and 10-pointers account for 30.77% of the cards). An *imbalanced* situation is where the cards do not reflect those proportions.

Any examination of the issue of imbalances in the game of blackjack, by the way, exposes one reason a Basic Strategy approach is woefully inadequate. Don't Old School Basic Strategy fanatics *admit* that *Basic Strategy is only correct if and when the cards are balanced?* But when is THAT?

To begin with, balance is mathematically impossible 50%

With Card Analysis: First Identify The Imbalances

of the time — when an odd number of cards are on the table! So, Basic, is, from the get-go, already wrong 50% of the time! Given the probability that imbalances will exist even with an even number of cards on the table, you should realize now that Basic has to -- from the stand-point of imbalances alone -- be wrong most of the time.

The earliest proponents of the late 20th Century's first computer-produced systems realized this. They warned you that Basic Strategy often did not provide the right move and so you needed to adjust your strategy through the use of a card counting system. This was their way of acknowledging *imbalances* that regularly throw off Basic Strategy's math-ematical logic. (Unfortunately, card counting has proven inadequate in identifying and responding to imbalances.)

Now -- getting back to the original idea I presented in this column -- how do imbalances affect the wisdom of your move? Why should you learn to identify them? Here's a simple example:

If you've got 11 points and the cards dealt so far include *four* 9s and *ten* 10s in the first round of a 2-deck table with 6 players, this imbalance is working against you. If you didn't pick up on it, you would probably make the wrong move. In this case, you should NOT double down, no matter what the up card is.

Why? If this were a balanced situation, there would be at most *two* 9s on the table and *six* 10s — by *the end* of the round!

How can I say that? The average number of cards dealt at a 6-player table is 19 -- less than two suits of cards. There-fore, the 9 being just one card in each suit, would appear once or twice in this mix, at most, in a balanced situation. The number of 10s by the round's end is equal to the num-ber of players at the table, in a balanced situation.

So, we've identified an *imbalance* that tells you there is a lower-than-normal proportion of 9s and 10s among the *undealt* cards. This imbalance tells you a number of things:

1. The two most desirable cards you'd want to get when doubling on your 11 are less likely to fall on your hand than normal.

2. If you're less likely to get a 9, which would give you a strong score of 20, and you're less likely to get a 10, which would give you the highest winning score, 21, then you're not likely to compete well against the dealer's probable score. (Already, your *best* hope now is to achieve a top score of 19, which is just the average winning score, and not a great competitor.)

3. Of the eight cards that you are most likely to get – the Ace, 2, 3, 4, 5, 6, 7, and 8 – FIVE would give you a stiff (a score of 12 through 16, where the dealer would have to bust for you to win), and two (the 6 and 7) would give you a sub-par winning score (the average winning score, again, being 19).

4. The dealer's hole card is not likely to be a 9 or 10, therefore the dealer is less likely to bust with his or her weakest up cards (the 4 through 6).

The imbalance we've identified in this example tells you that *doubling* your outlay while limiting yourself to one hit card makes little sense. Get it?

This shows you why, if you want to play blackjack with precision, you need to get in touch with the *imbalances* that exist during any given round. It's not very hard to pull off.

Just look at what's on table and see what cards are over-represented and what cards are under-represented and ask yourself: 1) What does that mean with regard to the hand I'm holding?; and, 2) What does that mean with regard to the dealer's likely hole card?

Doing Card Analysis In Spite Of Those Facedown Cards

'Got a postcard from a loyal reader of my syndicated column, Martin Deschner, who wrote:

The 1- & 2-deck games seem bad for the card analyst, as the first 2 player cards are hidden. You want to see as many cards as possible [to make smart card strategy decisions].

Martin, thankfully, that's no longer a problem. I introduced the world's first (and *only*) method to accurately identify the facedown cards at the 1- and 2-deck tables in *Cutting Edge Blackjack*. (Howard Schwartz, known as Las Vegas' "Librarian For Gamblers," especially praised that portion of *Cutting Edge Blackjack* in his review for Midwest Gaming & Travel Magazine, saying that I was the first blackjack innovator to identify the different *types* of facedown cards you need to know, and that my method for identifying them gives players a lot more *precision* in making card choices.)

If you've been avoiding those tables because of the facedown cards, you absolutely need to read that book (there are two chapters that explain how to go about it) – this is powerful stuff. The 1- and 2-deck games offer you your highest likelihood of success; and the action is much more predictable IF you know what the facedown cards are.

We can take a quick look at what this involves here. In order to figure out what the facedown cards most likely are, you need to understand that there are various *categories* of those cards. For example, *the cards players immediately stand on* form one category; *the cards players stand on after taking hit cards* form another. The composition of the cards in each category is very different. The cards players immediately stand on are unusually rich in *high* cards; the cards players stand on after taking hit cards are rich in *low* cards. (The makeup of these cards varies, though, depending on what dealer up card is on the table.) It all sounds complicated in a short column, but, at my seminars, I can teach this in about a half hour.

I'll give you one example not of my method itself, but how you might use the information I give you in *Cutting Edge Blackjack* regarding the facedown card categories to play a better game. Let's say you have 11 points; the dealer's up card is a 9; and the 6 other players at the table stand on their first two cards. Should you double? No way! *Hit*.

In *Cutting Edge*, I revealed that, when the dealer shows a 9, 60% of the First Category facedown cards are 10s and 26% are 8s and 9s (well above their normal proportions). This translates into a probability statement; the player with the 11 is far less likely than normal to get an 8, 9 or 10 as his hit card, so doubling would likely result in a loss here (the dealer achieves an average score of 18.86 with a 9).

The practice of requiring players to place their first two cards facedown on the table when standing at pitch games was instituted in the early 1960s, to make it hard for card counters to do their thing. In fact – that rule change all but made card counting ineffective at those tables... But, with my new method, that's no longer an impediment.

Beware The Old School Advice On Aces (Part 1)

In my most recent computer studies, I discovered many factors that led the blackjack researchers of the late 20th Century to reach faulty conclusions, which then resulted in their producing flawed methods.

In this column, let's look at how they went wrong regarding the effect Aces (or the lack of them) has on your ability to win. Once you read this chapter (and the next), I think you'll agree that you need to approach Aces in a new way.

The Old School approach which has dominated the blackjack world since it was created in 1961 advised you that, when Aces are overdue, you should raise your bet to the *maximum allowed amount*. The first book to introduce that idea was MIT math professor Edward Thorp's *Beat The Dealer*, based largely upon the work done by IBM's Julian Braun.

If truth be told, I believe that Braun's blackjack project was designed to promote IBM's machines. Also, please understand that neither Braun nor Thorp were blackjack players.

Thorp's total experience at the blackjack table consisted of two weeks, his bets funded entirely by two millionaires. At one point, Thorp wrote that he found himself down about $12,000! Even at today's currency valuations, $12K is a lot more money than the average player would want to lose. But, corrected for inflation, we see that Mr. Thorp's system led him to lose what would amount to over $250,000 today! I think on that basis alone you will realize that something is amiss with the Old School approach created by Messrs. Thorp and Braun.

Thorp clearly had a mistaken read on the value of Aces and it was because of the way he and Julian Braun went about doing their research -- as outlined in *Beat The Dealer*. Thorp said that in testing for the relative benefits of each type of card, "We watch the cards *that are used up on the first round of play*" [my italics]. To test Aces, he said, "...the *computer* was to do exactly the same thing it had done in finding the basic strategy, with one difference. It had to solve the problem with a *deck from which the four Aces were missing*."

First of all, his use of the word *deck* is misleading at best: *no cards were used in his research*. Julian Braun simulated blackjack action with his computer's *random number generator*. That unwittingly presented him with a major problem: *the cards do not play out randomly*, as any shuffle tracker or dealer can tell you!

His conclusion: "When playing *with a deck that has four Aces missing*, the player is at a disadvantage of 2.42 per cent."

What's wrong with all of this?

Number one, that tests only for the situation in which Aces are totally depleted. Most of the time, players face a far different situation – where at least *some* Aces are present.

Beware The Old School Advice On Aces (Part 1)

In addition, *Braun and Thorp ignored the situations where Aces are in play, and therefore should not have made any conclusions regarding their overall effect on things.*

I, instead, started my research with real cards. Only after the rounds were dealt was the computer allowed to analyze the results (this reflected the *realities* you face at the casino).

Then, I tested for how well players did when they received Aces, AND how well the *dealer* did versus the players when the dealer got an Ace, *because when Aces are due, the DEALER gets some too!*

(I also separated out the results vis a vis player blackjacks in one test of the Aces' value to players, which produced a very interesting revelation.)

This is the only way to do this kind of research, if you want the truth about who benefits the most from Aces – the player or the dealer!

In the next column, I'll reveal the true value of Aces, and why they benefit the dealer more than you. In the meantime: *do not raise your bet when Aces are due!*

Beware The Old School Advice on Aces (Part 2)

In the last column, I talked about how far adrift the researchers of the past 42 years have gone in their analysis of Aces and their benefit to the player.

I pointed out that, not only have these researchers conducted their studies in the wrong way (that is, they simulated the game with their computers' random number generators instead of starting with real blackjack action, with real cards, reflecting your reality at the blackjack table), but they then tested the value of Aces in the wrong way – by *removing the Aces* from play and studying the results on players' winning rates.

So how on Earth could they then say *anything* about how Aces work? For one thing, the early studies tested only for one-player situations, which fails to reflect the reality at multi-player tables. For another thing, they did not test for how *poorly* players do when the DEALER gets some of the Aces that are overdue – for, when Aces are overdue, the DEALER gets a goodly number of them, too!

Beware The Old School Advice on Aces (Part 2)

So, based upon this faulty research, the Old School researchers (some of whom are still operating today) then concluded (wrongly) that you should maximize your bet when Aces are overdue.

But, in fact, that's a great way of losing a lot of money, because Aces benefit the *dealer* more than you.

How did I come up with that conclusion? First, I conducted my research properly, by using real cards, dealt over the course of 2 years by real casino dealers (correctly reflecting your reality at the casino), and the results were then analyzed by a computer. This is the only way to start with correct data.

Next, to correctly determine the effect of Aces on a player's bottom line, I took all the data and removed the player hands that had no Aces EXCEPT in situations where the dealer, too, had an Ace.

Here's what I found, in a nutshell (if you want more details, the numbers are in *Cutting Edge Blackjack*): the only time Aces benefit you is when you get a blackjack.

One reason is that when you get an Ace without a blackjack the Ace in the mix actually causes you to reach a subpar average score over time and your score then competes poorly against the dealer's score.

Another reason is that the dealer's busting rate is ridiculously low when the dealer gets an Ace - either as the up card, hole card, third card, fourth card, or whatever. (Overall, the dealer's busting rate with an Ace in the mix is a miniscule 8 percent!) The flip side of that equation is: when the dealer does NOT get an Ace, the dealer's overall busting rate is in the forty percentile range!!! In fact, your gains, when the dealer does not get an Ace, will be nearly three times above average!!!

And that's based solely upon wins and losses - that doesn't even include the additional gains you'd experience by raising your bets intelligently!!! Because, as you can see now, the time to raise your bet dramatically is *when Aces are not likely to fall into the dealer's hands.*

When would this be? When Aces are entirely or almost entirely played out.

I know this runs contrary to what you've read in Old School books, but, tell me this: now that you know how they did their research and how I did my research, whose conclusions do you trust?!

Where Should You Place
The Cut Card?
(Part One)

A reader, Greg B., sent me this letter with these questions related to 1- and 2-deck games:

1. *Where should the cut card be placed to keep a good pattern repeating?*

2. *And, conversely, if the pattern is favoring the dealer, can the cards be cut so as to bring better cards into play, or should I just leave the table?*

3. *Does the placement of the cut card in a 6-deck shoe matter as much as in a 1- or 2-deck game?*

The correct placing of the cut card is one of blackjack's biggest mysteries for most players. (The cut card, for those who don't know, is the plastic card a player places in the newly-shuffled cards, to determine where the dealer will start dealing.)

Many players believe there's no way to know where to place the cut card, so they resort to audibly praying to the blackjack gods as they randomly stick it in the cards. Most players wind up placing it in the middle of the stack; some place it toward the top or bottom, often muttering: "Cut thin to win."

Random cutting doesn't accomplish anything. You're relying upon luck and that doesn't work very often. In fact, there are ways to cut the cards intelligently and effectively.

Unfortunately, cut card placement requires advanced skills. Before you know where to place it, you have to know something about shuffle tracking – this is where you keep track of the cards through a shuffle so you know roughly where they are in the newly-shuffled stack.

Nevertheless, I'll give you a few pointers that don't require shuffle tracking, and then, in the next column, I'll give you some shuffle tracking and more advanced cut-card-placement advice.

Let's start by looking at Greg B.'s questions.

Answer to Question #1: Without shuffle tracking skills (which would give you much more precision), the only way to hope to keep a good pattern going for a beginner is to place the cut card approximately where it was placed the last time the cards were cut. Because shuffling doesn't change the order of the cards that much, this tactic often works.

Answer to Question #2: This is a harder question to answer. If the problem is that the general mix of cards is bad, no amount of card cutting will make them good; your best move would be to leave the table and find a better one. If the problem is a short run of bad cards, then you'd want to place the cut cards in an area away from that problem section, but that requires shuffle tracking techniques (which we'll discuss next time).

Answer to Question #3: Any and every advantage you have produces greater gains for you in blackjack; you want every edge. So, yes, if you know what you're looking for, then you can cut the cards to your advantage, no matter how

Where Should You Place The Cut Card? (Part Two)

many decks are in play. Obviously, it's easier to keep track of the cards in a pitch game (a 1- or 2-deck game, in which the dealer holds the cards in his or her hand) than in a shoe game (a game with more than 2 decks, in which the cards are to be found in a plastic box on the table). But, yes, if there was a long string of good cards in a 6-deck game, you'd want to cut the cards to bring them back in the early rounds after the shuffle — then, you could raise your bet to take advantage of what you know is likely to occur, in a situation where you'd otherwise be cautious.

More next time.

Where Should You Place The Cut Card? (Part Two)

In the last column, I gave reader Greg B. some answers regarding the questions he sent, namely:

1. *Where should the cut card be placed to keep a good pattern repeating?*

2. *If the pattern is favoring the dealer, can the cards be cut so as to bring better cards into play (or should you leave the table)?*

A player needs to acquire *card analysis* and *shuffle tracking* skills before he or she can answer these questions accurately, because the answers depend upon what I call the unique personality of the cards you're facing and the shuffling style of the casino.

Let's talk briefly about the card analysis portion of this equation today.

Card analysis requires that you develop keen powers of observation (and *know* what you're looking for). In Question 2, for instance, Greg talks about bad patterns that favor the dealer.

Where Should You Place The Cut Card? (Part Two)

Let's examine this. There are many different types of bad patterns.

Actually, we should distinguish between "patterns" and "mixes" first. A "pattern" is an ordering of the cards that appears in a significant portion of the pile, if not the whole enchilada. A "mix" is a more general term: it's the way the cards wind up after the shuffle, and, most often, it does not contain an identifiable "pattern." A mix has card imbalances, however, that you look for – some are good, some bad.

Through card analysis, you need to identify which type you're facing – a "pattern" or "mix" — and whether card cutting can change things for the better.

This is a rather advanced skill, but I'll give you a for-instance: say the cards come out in a high-low-high-low-high-low *pattern* (you see a King and then a 6, then a 9 and a 5, then a 10 and a 4, and so on). This is terrible; it often results in stiff hands for players (hands of 12-16 points that bust too often). You cannot alter this pattern by cutting the cards creatively. If you spot this, you should leave the table.

Another type of bad pattern is one that results from incomplete shuffling from the get-go. You can spot this easily: most, if not all cards in one or two suits (depending on the number of players at the table) will appear in one round, and each subsequent round. Sometimes the cards will even be dealt sequentially. If you see this, *leave the table*.

Now, on the other hand, if the general mix of cards results in too many dealer blackjacks, you might be able to cut the cards to prevent this from happening again. To do this, you need to watch where the Aces wind up in the discard pile. (Often, they'll be in a position that lends to easy tracking through the shuffling process.)

Then, you should visually follow the Aces through the shuffle and place the cut card so that it's BELOW those Aces

— so those Aces end up in the portion that will NOT get dealt.

Any intelligent card cutting process requires that you keep track of where significant cards (cards you want to follow) wind up in the discard pile — because that determines where they'll wind up AFTER the shuffle. This is a basic skill you must develop if you want to get into shuffle tracking and intelligent card cutting.

So, the answers to Greg's questions lie in a player's ability to: 1) spot card mixes that are either favorable or not (and determine whether bad mixes can be cut out); 2) bookmark card locations in the discard pile; and 3) follow them through the shuffle - this is what I'll talk about in my next column.

Shuffle Tracking 101:
How Riffling
Reorders The Cards

Following cards through the shuffle is not as hard as you'd think. I teach the rudiments, with a deck of cards, in half an hour at my seminars. (You should seek out games where the cards are hand-shuffled, of course; and, preferably, 1- and 2-deck games.)

Now, every casino has a slightly different shuffling procedure. Shuffling procedures are standardized (done the same way each time), and consist of at least two types of shuffles. The dealer's skill and discretion also affect the outcome somewhat.

One type of shuffle you'll *always* see done in a casino's shuffling procedure is the *riffle*. That's the kind of shuffle everyone learns as a child.

The riffle begins with the dealer cutting the cards in two; good dealers can often cut them exactly in half, as shown in the chart on page 103. A skilled dealer then will knit one card from each side together, from the bottom on up, until the cards are together again.

I've labeled the 13 cards that were on top before the dealer cut the cards "TOP;" the 13 that were below those, "MIDDLE/TOP;" the 13 that were below those, "MIDDLE/BOTTOM;" and the 13 below those, "BOTTOM." See what's going to happen?* **The TOP cards will stay on top. The BOTTOM cards will remain at the bottom. The MIDDLE/TOP will gravitate to the** *bottom* **half, and the MIDDLE/BOTTOM will gravitate to the** *top* **half.**

Now, please understand that the skill level of the dealer determines how perfectly the cards are riffled together. **A very skilled dealer will do it so that formerly neighboring cards will be separated by just one or two cards per riffle. With less skilled dealers, formerly neighboring cards might wind up separated by three or more cards per riffle.** You should watch the process closely to see for yourself how this plays out, to adjust your assessment as to where the cards wind up after the riffle.

Also, most dealers start the riffle off slowly and then speed up as they get closer to the top. This often results in the topmost cards being less perfectly sewn together -- in other words, more than one card would tend to wind up falling from one half before cards of the other half have been added to the mix. Look carefully to see if this might be happening, in estimating where the cards wind up in the end.

Study the chart on the next page carefully. Depending on where the cards you want to keep track of are, you should now have a good idea where they will be following a riffle.

Next time: stripping.

---

*Let me explain what's going on in the chart on the next page. These are the two halves the dealer is about to riffle together. If he or she starts the riffle with the right half, for instance, the riffle would go like this: card #52 will be laid on the table, then card #26, then card #51, card #25 and so on, until the two halves are back together as a whole.

Graphic Representation
of Riffling
(After Dealer Cutting Procedure)

#			#	
1	TOP		27	MIDDLE/BOTTOM
2	TOP		28	MIDDLE/BOTTOM
3	TOP		29	MIDDLE/BOTTOM
4	TOP		30	MIDDLE/BOTTOM
5	TOP		31	MIDDLE/BOTTOM
6	TOP		32	MIDDLE/BOTTOM
7	TOP		33	MIDDLE/BOTTOM
8	TOP		34	MIDDLE/BOTTOM
9	TOP		35	MIDDLE/BOTTOM
10	TOP		36	MIDDLE/BOTTOM
11	TOP		37	MIDDLE/BOTTOM
12	TOP		38	MIDDLE/BOTTOM
13	TOP		39	MIDDLE/BOTTOM
14	MIDDLE/TOP		40	BOTTOM
15	MIDDLE/TOP		41	BOTTOM
16	MIDDLE/TOP		42	BOTTOM
17	MIDDLE/TOP		43	BOTTOM
18	MIDDLE/TOP		44	BOTTOM
19	MIDDLE/TOP		45	BOTTOM
20	MIDDLE/TOP		46	BOTTOM
21	MIDDLE/TOP		47	BOTTOM
22	MIDDLE/TOP		48	BOTTOM
23	MIDDLE/TOP		49	BOTTOM
24	MIDDLE/TOP		50	BOTTOM
25	MIDDLE/TOP		51	BOTTOM
26	MIDDLE/TOP		52	BOTTOM

This had been the top half before the dealer cut.

This had been the bottom half before the dealer cut.

© 2004 by Richard Harvey

Shuffle Tracking 101: How Stripping Reorders The Cards

Stripping is a type of shuffle of which few players know the name, to which few pay much attention. It is, however, the second most likely type of dealer shuffle, after the common riffle, to be included during the shuffling procedure at most casinos. (In fact, perhaps the most common shuffling procedure nationwide is the riffle-riffle-strip-riffle sequence, which I abbreviate as R2SR.)

If you want to become a shuffle tracker, to know where to place the cut card when it's your turn, or to know whether good cards or bad cards are likely to come first as a result of someone else cutting the cards, you need to know how the various types of shuffles – riffling, boxing, stripping, washing, etc. – affect the order of the cards.

This skill can be a very profitable one. If you know what cards are likely to come after the shuffle, you can devise a more intelligent betting strategy. You'd raise your normal bet when good cards are coming first (to increase your profits), or lower it when bad cards are coming first (to minimize your risk). Or, you might even want to leave the

Shuffle Tracking: How Stripping Reorders The Cards

table if the cutting of the cards spells disaster.

Stripping is a process in which the dealer holds the cards in his or her left hand while his or her right hand rapidly takes cards in small clumps off the top and places them progressively in a new pile on the table. The chart on the next page shows you the result: cards formerly on top are now on the bottom, and cards that were on the bottom are now on the top. The cards in the middle are reversed in order.

So, if you wanted to follow four Aces that were on the very top of the pile before the stripping began, that's easy – they're now on the bottom. And vice versa.

Now, there are two types of stripping: severe or normal. With severe stripping, fewer cards are moved at one time; that makes it easier to follow the cards — the result is closer to an exact top-to-bottom reversal.

Combine all of this with what you learned about riffling, and you're on your way to making that much more money at blackjack. This is one of many ways you can profit from the non-random nature of the game.

THE EFFECT OF STRIPPING

New Order	Original Order	Original Position
1	45	BOTTOM
2	46	BOTTOM
3	47	BOTTOM
4	48	BOTTOM
5	49	BOTTOM
6	50	BOTTOM
7	51	BOTTOM
8	52	BOTTOM
9	38	MIDDLE/BOTTOM
10	39	MIDDLE/BOTTOM
11	40	BOTTOM
12	41	BOTTOM
13	42	BOTTOM
14	43	BOTTOM
15	44	BOTTOM
16	28	MIDDLE/BOTTOM
17	29	MIDDLE/BOTTOM
18	30	MIDDLE/BOTTOM
19	31	MIDDLE/BOTTOM
20	32	MIDDLE/BOTTOM
21	33	MIDDLE/BOTTOM
22	34	MIDDLE/BOTTOM
23	35	MIDDLE/BOTTOM
24	36	MIDDLE/BOTTOM
25	37	MIDDLE/BOTTOM
26	19	MIDDLE/TOP
27	20	MIDDLE/TOP
28	21	MIDDLE/TOP
29	22	MIDDLE/TOP
30	23	MIDDLE/TOP
31	24	MIDDLE/TOP
32	25	MIDDLE/TOP
33	26	MIDDLE/TOP
34	27	MIDDLE/BOTTOM
35	11	TOP
36	12	TOP
37	13	TOP
38	14	MIDDLE/TOP
39	15	MIDDLE/TOP
40	16	MIDDLE/TOP
41	17	MIDDLE/TOP
42	18	MIDDLE/TOP
43	1	TOP
44	2	TOP
45	3	TOP
46	4	TOP
47	5	TOP
48	6	TOP
49	7	TOP
50	8	TOP
51	9	TOP
52	10	TOP

Dealing Brings
The Cards
Back Together

When *Blackjack The SMART Way* first came out, some Old School writers questioned my assertion that the cards had a "personality" that persisted from shuffle to shuffle. The same happened when I announced in *Cutting Edge Black-jack* that I had discovered *that repeating* phenomena could be identified from shuffle to shuffle -- repeating hole cards, dealer up cards, player cards, whole groups of cards, etc.

But the Old School writers could not have known about such things because their books were based on antiquated, decades-old computer research that relied upon their com-puters' *random number generators* to *simulate* blackjack rounds to produce data. Because no cards were used, and because the simulated "cards" were produced *randomly*, the researchers behind the Old School books falsely concluded that real cards behave *randomly*.

Nothing could be further from the truth. In my most recent computer research studies, I demonstrated how cards *really* behave. And, aside from the repeating phe-nomena I have documented beyond a doubt, I want to show you just one operating principle that makes the cards stay pretty much the same from shuffle to shuffle. I don't believe this has been identified by anyone else -- I certainly haven't seen this in any other blackjack book.

Namely: **shuffling separates cards that were together in the same hand somewhat by placing cards in between former neighbors;** *DEALING tends to bring them back together!* I'll show you how.

For example: let's say one player had a blackjack...an A♥ and a J♣... prior to the shuffle...and let's say the dealer's shuffling inserted four cards between this pair.

If you look at the illustration at the top of the next page, *you can see how easily this blackjack might come back together in the same hand because of the dealing process* (this example illustrates how it would happen at a four-player table).

The cards being dealt are represented by the list on the left. The numbers on each card correlate with the order in which they were dealt. On the game board you can see how this order would result in the A♥ and J♣ coming back together, in the first baseman's hand.

If you previously suspected some repeating mechanism was afoot in the game of blackjack, this confirms your suspicions (but it's just part of the story — for *details* on how to profit from repeating phenomena and casino shuffling practices, see *Cutting Edge Blackjack*). Many players take notice of this on some level, for instance, when the order of the cards seems to give one player most of the player blackjacks through many shuffles (this is usually due to card repetition).

This reminds me of the dealer in Las Vegas who told me the story of the shuffling machine he noticed was dealing the exact same cards, in *the exact same order,* after a shuffle as had been dealt in the prior shuffle period! The

Dealing Brings The Cards Back Together

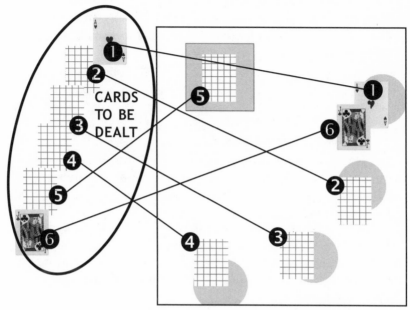

machine was broken and nobody noticed it except for him,
he asserted. The players were getting the same cards
following a "shuffle" that they had gotten prior to the
"shuffle." (I put shuffle in quotes, because he assumed the
machine was not really shuffling, when it should have been.)
I laughed along with him -- we both detested shuffling
machines.

But, something about his story bothered me, and for days
I kept trying to figure out what was wrong with it. Finally,
one day, I figured out what was probably going on.

That machine could *not* have been broken. If it had NOT
been shuffling at all, players would not have gotten the
same cards as they had before the shuffle. **The illustration
above proves that, for players to have gotten the same
cards after the shuffle, shuffling would have had to
have taken place. Cards equal to the total number of
players at the table would have had to have been
placed between cards formerly dealt to one player.**

Now, I had a clue in that the dealer told me *the shuffling machine at his table was performing seven riffles per shuffle.* So, *seven cards were likely being inserted between cards that had formerly been together in one hand.* At a seven-player table, this could have produced the same repeating effect you saw in the illustration on the prior page, if the first card to be dealt from the machine was the same as it was in the prior shuffle period. (And perhaps ALL of the cards didn't come out exactly as the dealer had recalled; just enough to indicate to him that a large-scale repeating phenomenon was going on.) What the dealer had discovered was NOT that the machine was broken, but that *the cards stay largely the same from one shuffle period to another because of the phenomenon I mentioned before. Shuffling separates formerly neighboring cards somewhat and dealing tends to bring those cards back together in much the same order they were in before, such that the action doesn't change significantly.*

I first noticed that standardized casino dealer shuffling doesn't change things very much when I was playing one evening at Foxwoods in Connecticut (purportedly the largest casino in the world). When they first opened, there were quite a number of inexperienced dealers working there -- one of whom was at my table, this particular night. It was obvious to me that this dealer hadn't shuffled the new cards that were brought to the table very well -- from observing her shuffle, and from seeing the results when she dealt the cards. The cards came out of the shoe largely in clumps of whole suits (in other words, most if not all of two suits would appear on the table by the end of each round).

But that isn't what was so astonishing.

When she shuffled the cards after our first shuffle period with these new cards, *the cards again came out as they had before* -- in clumps of whole suits. My observation of this phenomenon -- the repetition of large clumps of cards from shuffle to shuffle -- was an Epiphany. It took me years, however, to uncover exactly what was going on (in other words, that shuffling does not reorder the cards much, and, as you saw here, that dealing then brings the cards back together much as they were before).

You've read it here first. The best thing about it is that *this nonrandom reality about blackjack will enable you to play a better game and win more.*

What does this tell you? Many things. But, especially that what I said before about the cards having a personality that repeats from shuffle to shuffle is true.

What does this mean to you?

1) For one thing, it means you should never assume your luck is going to change when you're at a bad table. Aside from the fact that luck has nothing to do with winning at blackjack, what you've just seen shows you that bad cards tend to stay bad cards. If things are really bad, your best option is to leave the table.

2) For another, once you get good at identifying how good or bad the cards are from shuffle to shuffle, you can adjust your bets accordingly (putting more money on the table the better the cards).

3) And finally, that you should be *looking* for repeating patterns characteristic to each set of cards you face and for how well the table is doing in general, so that you have a good idea of what's coming after the shuffle, good or bad.

As you've just seen -- unlike what some Old School writers would have you believe -- **you can predict with good certainty what's to come following the dealer's shuffling of the cards based upon what you saw in the previous shuffle period.**

Strategic Stacking: You Always Count Your Money

"You never count your money when you're sittin' at the table...There'll be time enough for countin' when the game is through." - Kenny Rogers' "The Gambler"

I'll buy the line in the song about "you've got to know when to fold up," but, for blackjack players, I disagree about the rest of the quote above. Counting your money at the table is something you MUST do, on a *continual* basis.

I get the feeling that many players are shy about keeping an accurate running count. Perhaps they're afraid it might make them seem like greenhorns. Or they might be out to impress others with their recklessness. How foolish. Others simply don't understand the importance of doing so.

Let's take a look at just some of the reasons why you need to perform a little ritual I call Strategic Stacking, to easily keep track of your chips at all times, at a glance.

At my seminars, I sometimes show a video (from a video

Strategic Stacking: You Always Count Your Money

surveillance camera) of a high roller sitting at a blackjack table with his many chips in disarray. A woman with a coffee cup asks the man if she can touch his chips with her cup, to bring herself some of his good luck. The man nods yes, and, as the woman walks away, so does one of the man's $100 chips (unbeknownst to him). She'd used double-stick tape on the bottom of her cup to steal a chip! Luckily, someone in the surveillance room had noticed the scam and recouped the man's loss.

Why hadn't the man realized he'd been ripped off? He hadn't stacked his chips properly, so he had no idea one was missing after the cup trick.

At another casino, I watched as a man who had carelessly stacked his chips was about to walk out with $25 less than he should have. He was coloring in* before leaving and the dealer had made five stacks out of the man's red $5 chips, and was getting ready to pay him $125 (and the man was about to accept that amount and leave).

What was wrong with that? *The dealer had placed six chips in each stack!* The man actually had $150. When coloring in a player, a dealer should place five $5 chips in each stack – that's the convention; and, in fact, she was about to pay him off as if she had done so! *The man wasn't aware of the mistake, because he hadn't kept track of how many chips he'd had!* (The pit boss noticed the mistake and spared the man the $25 loss.)

Those are just two examples of how sloppy bookkeeping can lead to trouble. But there are other reasons to keep a constant reckoning of what you have.

For instance – how would you know if you're up or down if you don't know at any given time what you have? And, if you don't know if you're up or down, how do you know: 1) how to bet; and 2) when it's time to leave? These are

---

*Coloring in = the dealer exchanging players' low value chips for higher value chips when possible, so the table does not run out of low chips.

two crucial decisions that should take into account whether you're winning or losing, and by how much.

In *Cutting Edge Blackjack* I introduced my computer research discovery that, by keeping track of your relative number of wins and losses, you can mathematically determine your likelihood of doing better or worse (and therefore know: how to bet, and when it's time to leave). But how can you do so if you don't always know what you have?

Here's my advice; you should do what I call *Strategic Stacking*:

If you are using $5 chips, place them in front of you in piles of five chips, so each pile equals $25. That way, you see four piles, it's $100, five piles, it's $125, and so on -- it's a snap to see what you have.

If you are using $25 chips, stack them in piles of four, so each pile equals $100. If you're using $100 chips, make piles of five chips, so each stack equals $500. And so on.

(If you have an odd number of chips, ones that are left-over after making your standard-size stacks, use these to begin a new stack.)

This way, your chips are working for you. They spell out quickly how much you have. And you don't have to waste time or distract yourself by physically counting each chip.

Strategic Stacking gives you a visual cue as to what you have, so you can instantly compare what you have at any time to what you brought and know whether you're up or down, and by how much. It lets you safeguard your winnings; you can easily earmark what you want to take home with you, so you never go back below a certain level. It also aids you in making other crucial decisions, such as deciding when you should leave (whether up or down).

Finally, Strategic Stacking is great in that it lets you accomplish all of this without being obvious about it.

Loss Limits
& How To
Avoid Big Trouble

At one of my book signing events at a major bookstore, a woman told me she'd been in a casino where a man shot himself to death after losing a lot of money at the blackjack table. On a different day, at a post office, a man told me he was really upset that he'd lost $300 at a $5 table (which he considered a big loss).

These stories represent flip sides of the same coin.

You need to understand the concept of *loss limits*. This is key to becoming a winner. More important, it is key to avoiding big trouble.

First, let's dispel some common misconceptions. Please understand that:

1. *Every player experiences losing sessions, no matter what system they use.* It's strange, but it doesn't seem as if many players are aware of this.

2. There is no system that can guarantee you x amount of dollars in winnings per hour (although some claim to). This

faulty thinking leads you to play longer than is wise, which results in high losses.

3. Luck has nothing to do with blackjack. Therefore, the "my luck is about to change" syndrome is a prescription for big trouble.

4. Making larger and larger bets in a desperate attempt to recoup big losses will result in disaster.

There are many reasons why you might find yourself losing. They are too many to go into here, but know this – at a 7-player table, there will be, *on average* 3 winners, one player who stays just about even, and 3 losers. This is the way the cards play out, under clinical conditions. If you're in one of those losing betting spots, you're looking for trouble if you stay there too long. This concept – a unique result of my computer studies of card behavior – cannot be stressed enough.

Ask any poker player about bad cards. In fact, that Kenny Rogers poker song that says "you need to know when to fold up" is also true for blackjack!

That's where loss-limits come into play. In *Cutting Edge Blackjack*, I've given you a scientific means of knowing when you've reached the "point of no return" in terms of losses — the stage at which your probability of coming back to even is practically nil.

That is beyond the scope of a short column. But, I will give you a method that a beginner can use to avoid large losses. The basic concept is: *don't allow your average losing day to eclipse any one winning day*. This is real important. I'll spell this out in detail in a moment. First, you need to understand this:

In pre-publication tests, my *Blackjack The SMART Way* system was shown to have a win rate of 88%. That means, it won on 88 of 100 trips to the casino. But that only told part of the story. On 12 of 100 trips, losses were incurred.

Loss Limits & How To Avoid Big Trouble

If those losing trips were not managed properly, the net result might still be *negative*!

Now, you know what you win, on average, on winning days – you can you this as a guide, if you'd like.

Or, consider this: beginners who use my Basic Strategy and 3-Level, Notch-Up, Notch-Down Bet Management System should see winning days that fall into a range of 20- to 40-times their minimum bet, on average. If that reflects your typical results, here's my suggestion if you have no loss limits in place right now: *once your losses have become greater than 10 times your minimum bet, leave.*

Everyone experiences losing days. How you handle these days is key to your becoming a winner.

State-of-the-Art Betting Strategies (Part 1)

When I was on the Mike Rosen show on KOA, a caller asked me what I thought about his betting system. He used what he called a negative progression system. He'd bet $25 in one round; then $40 in the next; then $60; then $100.

I asked him, "Why do you do that?" His response: "I dunno. That's what works for me." But it *cannot* work – unless the caller is sitting at one of those tables where the cards you get are so good you cannot help but win, whether you know how to play or not.

Number one, if you can't tell me why you're betting the way you do, you need to find a betting system that makes logical sense to you, so you know what you're doing with your money.

Number two, let's look at the caller's method closely. First off, it is rare when you would ever win four hands in a row, *no matter how good the table*. The odds are *against* that. Yet, his system *depends* upon this improbability. And, unless you're at *a good betting spot*, you'd have a less-than-50%

probability of winning three, let alone two hands in a row. To win much, his method requires that he win three hands in a row.

But, let's assume the caller did win three in a row. His odds of winning the fourth hand being less than 50%, he'll lose that $100 bet more than not. So, what would be the result, in this rosiest of cases?

He bets $25 (so his stash of chips outside the betting spot is now lower than when he started, by $25); however, he wins this $25 bet. He then takes $10 in chips from the profits and puts this back in his stash; he places the rest of his winnings, $15, on top of the $25 he risked initially. So – since his stash went down $25 upon placing his first bet, and he only placed $10 back into it since then — if he loses the $40 bet, he'll actually be *down* $15 from when he started the progression. However, if he wins the $40 bet, he'll take $20 of the winnings and place it on his stash, or bankroll; he'll take the other $20 in winnings and place it atop the rest of the chips he's been risking. Because his stash was down $15 after the last round, with the addition of $20, it's now up $5. So, if he loses the $60 bet, he'll now be up just $5 from when he started his progression. However, let's say he wins the $60 bet. He'll place $20 of that on his bankroll, which is now up $25 from when he started; he'll take the rest of his winnings, $40, and let it ride on the next round, atop the pile of chips already in his betting spot. His next bet is, over time, going to be a big loser.

So let's say he loses the $100 bet. Where does that leave him? After four rounds he's up only $25. That's a small return for a run of three wins (which is a best-case scenario). Plus, why throw away $100 in profits on the last bet?

At best, the caller's strategy produces poor results. He is right about one thing: you cannot win much by flat betting (always betting the same amount). Using Old School Basic Strategy methods, your gains would be less than 1%. That's at a 1-deck table, under the *best* of conditions. More next.

State-of-the-Art
Betting Strategies
(Part 2)

In my most recent computer studies, I discovered cutting edge betting indicators that were proven highly effective in determining when you should raise or lower your bets – and when you should *leave* a table.

One of those indicators is something I have called your *Win/Loss Margin* (or WLM). This is basically how your wins stack up against your losses.

For example, if you've won three more hands than you've lost, then your Win/Loss Margin is +3. On the other hand, if you've *lost* three more hands than you've won, then your WLM is -3. And so on.

This is easy to keep track of at the table. You can use your chips, for example, as count indicators.

An interesting thing happened once I invented this idea, and tested it to see if it was a good predictor of things to come (which it is). I had an Epiphany. I decided to *graph* the progress of the virtual players who'd been dealt cards in

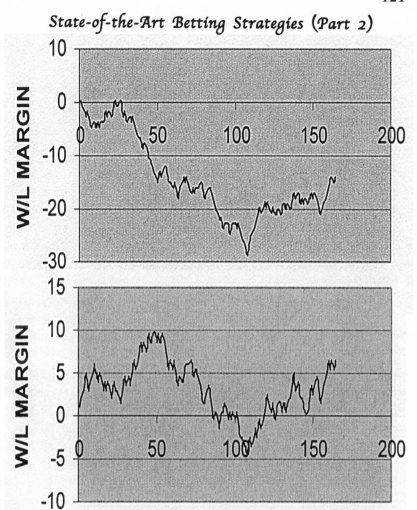

ROUNDS IN NUMERICAL ORDER

my research, based upon their WLM progress, from round to round.

As you can see above, the results looked like stock market charts. This revealed many things.

The charts above show the progress of two players *at the same table*. Can you detect any telling patterns?

There are three distinct periods reflected in both players'

charts. First there's a neutral period that lasts for about 25 rounds (neither player's WLM progresses much). Then, there's a down period of at least 50 rounds. Then, there's an up period of more than 50 rounds. (Player #2 enjoys an upswing, however, not experienced by Player #1.)

This proves that each set of cards exhibits a long-term personality that affects everyone at the table.

These charts also demonstrate that streaks *do* exist.

Now, looking at Player #1's losing streak of more than 75 rounds, can you see why the player who plays on despite a losing streak (believing "my luck has got to change!") is often sadly mistaken?

Can you also see why I caution players to make *minimum* bets when first arriving at a table until the cards break out from a neutral period (in terms of WLM numbers)?

State-of-the-Art
Betting Strategies
(Part 3)

Some blackjack writers seem intent on denying the existence of winning streaks. Others admit streaks exist but claim you cannot profit from them.

Look at the chart on the next page. The three columns on the left are from a pamphlet by a writer who wants you to believe that streaks do not exist. I added the two rightmost columns with information that's more telling.

There's a problem from the get-go with the writer's columns. His data was produced the Old School way – the researcher used his computer's *random* number generator to *simulate* blackjack action. Why would an intelligent person test the existence of streaks (*nonrandom* events) using a *random* device to create *pretend* data?

Studies from the 1970s on have shown that cards are *not* randomized by dealer shuffling. Additionally, my computer studies – which began with the casino-style shuffling and dealing of real cards – have turned up many types of *repeat-*

New Ways To Win MORE At Blackjack

	WRITER'S PAMPHLET		MY FIGURES	
# Wins in Streak	# Streaks Occurring	%	# Rounds In Streak (Col. 1 x Col. 2)	%
1	512	50.00%	512	25.01%
2	256	25.00%	512	25.01%
3	128	12.50%	384	18.76%
4	64	6.25%	256	12.51%
5	32	3.13%	160	7.82%
6	16	1.56%	96	4.69%
7	8	0.78%	56	2.74%
8	4	0.39%	32	1.56%
9	2	0.20%	18	0.88%
10	1	0.10%	10	0.49%
11	1	0.10%	11	0.54%
Totals:	1024		2047	74.99%

State-of-the-Art Betting Strategies (Part 3)

ing phenomena, from shuffle to shuffle.

So, using the data from the first three columns in the chart on the prior page is crazy. Interestingly, however, this researcher inadvertently discovered that streaks *do* exist. In fact, if you look at the rightmost column, it indicates that *a player's wins will occur during a winning streak 75% of the time* (summing the winning streaks of 2 or more)!

Now look at the graph below, reflecting just one players' progress from my study of real card behavior. Not only does it prove that streaks exist, it shows they tend to come in clumps, or *streaks* of streaks.

And you *can* profit from winning streaks. For instance, after a thorough analysis of winning streaks, I can tell you that once your wins outnumber your losses by 5, you will have a 63% probability of going up to 8 more wins than losses, and *your average mean peak will be at nearly 12 more wins than losses.*

Isn't that profitable information? *Wouldn't you raise your bet heading into such a likely situation?*

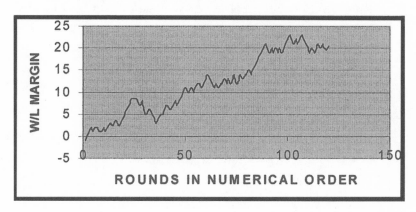

State-of-the-Art Betting Strategies (Part 4)

In recent columns, we talked about winning streaks and smart betting. Let's summarize some important points and then I'll give you a couple of suggestions on how to bet more wisely.

You've learned that winning streaks do occur. Most players understand this; they see it with their own eyes. I don't know why so many blackjack writers deny their existence. According to my computer research data, *a player's wins will occur during a winning streak roughly 70% of the time. Most* wins occur during a streak! You also saw in the last column how winning streaks tend to come in clumps — streaks of streaks.

Actually, to be frank, if it were not for winning streaks, few blackjack players would be winners. There are not that many skilled players, and most depend upon getting winning hands (such as blackjacks and hands of 20 and 21 points) to win.

State-of-the-Art Betting Strategies (Part 4)

It's not so rare to experience streaks of good cards from which you can profit. For blackjack players who haven't yet adopted a good betting system, let me give you a few suggestions on how to detect and profit from these positive trends. (One reason positive trends in blackjack often exist, by the way, is because of repeating phenomena I've discovered, phenomena that exist because dealer shuffling doesn't change the order of the cards that much. Each betting spot actually tends to get many of the same exact cards from shuffle to shuffle.)

Now, although I've developed more sophisticated betting techniques, here's what you can do:

Keep track of your Win/Loss Margin (WLM) - I taught you this recently. That's the number of your wins minus your losses.

There are many ways you can do this. You can keep a simple count with your chips — win one round, put one chip in front of your stash of chips, lose the next round, put it back on your stash (you're back to zero); lose a round, put a chip behind your stash (you're at -1); etc. Or, you can tap your chips rhythmically: tap-tap to the left means you're up two, tap-tap to the right means you're *down* two…You know…whatever works for you.

Then, you'll have a better idea of when you're at a good table. Your Win/Loss Margin (my invention) has proven to be a good indicator of how well you will do going into the future (due to the repeating card phenomena). There are other indicators, but let's concentrate on this one for now.

Once you get up to +5 WLM Units, for instance, my research shows that you're likely to achieve a mean average peak of nearly 12 Units. (This is for 1- and 2-deck games, by the way. Shoe games, games involving more than 2 decks, are harder to win at, and the average recreational player would do better to avoid them.)

So, when you reach +5, double your bet.

For those who want to be more aggressive at that point, raise your bet even further if you win a round. If you're timid, it's OK to raise your bet by just a portion of what you've won. For example, if you've won $20, you can place $10 of that back in your betting spot, and put the other $10 in your stash.

It's smart to do so, because *once you've gone over +5 Win/Loss Margin (WLM) Units, you're more than likely to have a second win following another.* Now, for the conservative: after that second win, reduce your bet back to whatever level you'd raised it to when you reached +5 WLM Units.

This approach, although not as profitable as my more sophisticated methods, is based upon sound thinking and yet it's conservative enough for beginners to pull off.

When To Take Insurance

When it comes to knowing when to take Insurance, most players are in the dark. Bullies will often try to dissuade you from taking Insurance saying "it's a bad bet." Their know-it-all attitude actually convinces some players that the bullies *know* what they are talking about. But they don't.

First of all, I'd like to know where the bullies got that mistaken notion. Dealers often tell players that Insurance is foolish; is this where this "gospel" comes from? It certainly doesn't come from blackjack's better books, by researcher/players.

Edward O. Thorp, who introduced the first computer-research-produced blackjack strategy in *Beat The Dealer* (1961), told you to take Insurance when the ratio of non-Tens to Tens falls below 2. Blackjack's Old School bullies never seem to remember this fact.

It wouldn't take much under Thorp's guidelines to achieve the condition calling for Insurance. For instance, if you're at a 1-deck, 2-player table, and you and the player next to you received four non-Tens as your first two cards with the dealer showing an Ace in the first round, Thorp would have you take Insurance.

The point I'm making is that Insurance has long been recognized as a good tool when card imbalances give the dealer a higher-than-average probability of having a 10 in the hole. (I am not endorsing the Thorp method, by the way. For one thing, it's a practical impossibility to pull off. How many players can keep track of the *exact* number of 10s and non-10s dealt – at every point – and then *divide* the number of non-10s by the number of 10s therefore determined to be in the *undealt* cards, to come up with precise two-decimal-point results?)

The reasoning behind the bullies' anti-Insurance stance is that 10-pointers account for just 31% of the cards, so therefore it's unlikely the hole card is a 10. (Incidentally, many of these same bullies are using faulty old systems that taught them to "always assume the hole card is a 10" – an interesting anomaly!). Yes, but that wisdom only pertains to the cards *before they were dealt,* or when they're *balanced.* As I mentioned in a prior column, smart blackjack players analyze the cards and adjust their card strategy to fit the current card *imbalances* – which have, from the time of Thorp on, been recognized to make Basic Strategy recommendations worthless. Thorp was telling you *there are often imbalances that make Insurance mathematically wise.*

The thing is: if you know the dealer likely has a 10 in the hole, you'd be crazy NOT to take Insurance. (I once had an ill-informed bully scoff at my taking Insurance, asking me incredulously: "you're insuring a *13*?" He didn't understand that by taking Insurance you're protecting your money from a certain loss, so *the composition of your hand doesn't matter.* The dealer indeed had a blackjack, and I was the only one at the table who knew this was likely and protected his bet.)

When To Take Insurance

So when do you take Insurance*? This goes back to my columns on how to identify the hole card, but here's an additional quick tip (a discovery I made in my last computer research project): *the number of 10s on the table should by round's end equal the number of betting spots being played.* So, if the number of 10s dealt is well below what you'd expect with those guidelines, the hole card is that much likelier to be a 10, and, therefore, Insurance is a wise move.

---

*To take Insurance, simply put a bet equal to half your original bet in the Insurance betting circle when the dealer asks, "Insurance?"

Smart Tipping
Can Increase
Your Winning Rate

It's amazing how many things you can do to win at black-jack. For instance, let's look at the much-overlooked factor of *tipping.*

Tipping (or *toking*) can be a useful strategic tool when used properly. Dealers don't make much (sometimes, just minimum wage), so tips can be used to tempt them to help you out.

For instance, one time, after sitting down to the right of the third baseman at a 1-deck table in Vegas with 6 boister-ously happy players, the third baseman leaned over and whispered to me: "We're tipping the dealer every hand!"

I understood what he meant. They were getting something special from the dealer that was helping them win, the tokes greasing the way to that end. So, I placed a $1 tip as a bet for the dealer. (I didn't know exactly what I'd be getting in return; I later made $5 tips!)

It didn't take long for me to see why the players were doing this. The dealer was giving them *two* rounds of action in each shuffle period. (The norm at this casino, I later found out, was to give just one round of action to tables of 6 or 7 players before shuffling up.)

What a tremendous edge the dealer was giving us! That meant I'd see about 40 or more cards before my turn in the second round! Talk about predictability! I'd know pretty well what cards remained undealt by my turn! Therefore, I'd know whether the dealer was likely to bust or score; whether the card(s) I'd need for successful doubling or splitting were in good number; whether taking a hit card would bust me; and, whether a hit card would give me a score competitive against the dealer's likely score.

For instance, if I'd had an 11 versus the dealer's 9 but there were just two 10-point cards among 10 undealt cards, the rest of which being 7s or lower, I wouldn't have doubled down. I wouldn't double my outlay with the likelihood of drawing to a paltry 17 or 18 or, worse yet, a stiff against the 9's strength. That's a losing proposition!

OK. So that's one instance of smart tipping.

You can sometimes encourage the dealer to give you a second round at a 1-deck game through tipping, by the way. Try this ruse: place a toke in the form of a bet after the 1st round, and then remove it if the dealer shuffles instead of giving you the second round. After the shuffle, try this one more time. The dealer might then give you your second round, knowing your tip is contingent upon your getting that extra round!

Another time, I was at a 2-deck table with three other players and the dealer had only dealt a few (devastating) rounds when she said something like "the cards are really bad; let's see if I can make that change." She then shuffled up way before the reshuffle card had been reached!

I immediately placed a $1 chip next to my bet to ride with mine as a tip for her with the next round. She had done something extraordinary to help us do better! You reward a gesture like that with a tip, so the dealer feels appreciated and is motivated to continue to act on your behalf.

I favor toking in the form of a bet, to give the dealer a reason to care about your success. However, you might consider giving an exceptionally helpful dealer a $5 or greater chip just before they leave the table. That's an investment for the future. He or she will remember you kindly the next time they deal to you and might therefore do something to tip things in your favor.

Report From Vegas:
Blackjack Variants
To Avoid

In *Blackjack The SMART Way*, I warned you not to play any of the blackjack variants because *there's always a catch.* Here, I'll go into more detail in discussing some of the blackjack offshoots I recently encountered in Las Vegas, of dubious merit.

For example: Spanish 21. This blackjack variant offers some tantalizing options including surrender. The only problem is the pips have been removed (the 10-pointers that say "10" on them). You must therefore adjust your card strategy if you want to deal with that imbalance properly, but few players realize that. (Hint: if you must play this game, use my Ducks & Bucks system to figure out how strong or weak the dealer is; if you highlight the ones that result from a deficit in 10s, and memorize the correct altered strategies per each up card, you'll play a much better game of Spanish 21.)

Another blackjack variant is Single Deck Super Fun 21. I picked up a promotional brochure on it at a major Las

Vegas Strip casino this week, and here's what it says:

1. Player may double down on any number of cards, even after splitting and hitting, including aces.

2. Player may split equal valued cards, including Aces, up to three times for a total of four hands.

3. Player may surrender one half of bet on any number of cards totaling less than 21, even after hitting, splitting or doubling down.

4. Any hand totaling 20 or less with six cards pays even money instantly.

5. Any hand totaling 21 with five or more cards pays 2-to-1 instantly.

6. *Any player's blackjack is an instant winner. Blackjack in diamonds pays 2-to-1; any other blackjack pays even money.*

Did you notice the catch at the end of that (I wonder how many players pick up on it)? *Most blackjacks pay only even money.* That results in a disadvantage of 3%.

The most *important* catch was NOT listed, however: players LOSE on pushes. This results in an additional 7% disadvantage.

Therefore, with Super Fun 21, *you're starting off with a 10% disadvantage over the typical standard blackjack game.*

Do you gain anything in return?

The ability to double on hands of three or more cards is tempting, but its advantages are fractional.

Being able to split Aces up to three times is wonderful, but how often does this really occur (therefore, the advantage gained here is questionable)?

Surrendering nets an advantage of about 2 per cent, but you can find this option at standard blackjack tables if

Report From Vegas: Blackjack Variants To Avoid

you're smart enough to seek it out (the extra advantage offered here – that of being able to surrender ANY hand at ANY point is tempting, but, again, its benefits are fractional).

The additional bonus you'd get achieving hands of 20 or less with six cards will occur so infrequently it doesn't even deserve a mention here. The additional bonus you'd get with hands of 21 points with five or more cards will occur only .2% of the time.

Being paid for blackjacks when the dealer has one too gives you a gain of a mere .3%.

So you gain (at most) a total of 1% in advantages with Super Fun 21, while accruing 10% in disadvantages. The net loss over playing a standard blackjack game is about 9%. There are too many standard single and double deck blackjack games with better odds in Vegas to warrant playing this variant.

Yet another blackjack variant is Double Exposure. Here, BOTH of the dealer's cards are dealt face up. Great! But here's the *catch*: you *lose* when you *push* with the dealer, costing you 7% in disadvantages. Not worth the price, especially considering that few players really know enough about card analysis to adjust their card strategy properly with regard to what the dealer is showing.

I didn't find Digital 21 in Vegas, but I have seen it elsewhere, so I thought I'd mention it here. This is where players sit at a table where instead of a betting spot there's a computer monitor that displays a simulated blackjack situation. There are many drawbacks to this game.

One is rather subtle, but, if you watch the screen next to the dealer, it shows a simulated shuffle between each rounds (at least the games I watched not long ago did this). That means you cannot analyze the cards from round to round, as you would with a normal game with cards, to get a good read on what's likely to come in the next round. That removes a significant player advantage.

In other words, if you saw four Aces in one round (and you were playing a normal 1-deck game with cards), you'd know that no more Aces are left. Therefore, you'd raise your bet significantly, all things being equal (if you were following my system), knowing that your chances of winning just went up significantly. No such ability with Digital 21.

In addition, without a true shuffling of cards, there is no predictability from "shuffle" to "shuffle." True cards are not randomized with standardized dealer shuffling, and you can predict certain repeating events (a concept introduced in detail in *Cutting Edge Blackjack*) as well as perform shuffle tracking (to know where to put the cut card, or know whether good or bad cards are coming if someone else placed the cut card). No such ability in Digital 21, where the computer's random number generator is dealing cards randomly.

It should be clear to you that none of the blackjack variants now available make things *better* for you. So, take my advice and stick to the real game.

The Latest Threat
To The Game:
Mindplay

Spying on players with 14 cameras...using invisible ink to mark cards so those cameras can tell what cards each player has gotten...using those cameras to record, in real time, players' card strategies and betting patterns. It sounds like something from a James Bond movie, but, sadly, it's the latest in a string of technological developments designed to make it harder for players to win at blackjack.

This particular technological marvel, MindPlay MP21, is now being touted in publicity articles as a great way to bounce card counters from the casino. The system is programmed to send an alert to casino surveillance monitoring employees when it detects a card counter. The way it does that is by checking to see if a players' bets go up dramatically when the card count becomes very positive, which is the strategy used by most counting systems born of the 1960s.

In a recent article, Richard Soltys, MindPlay CEO, asserted that his machines are practically *foolproof* in that way: "The chances of you actually playing in a way, by luck only, that matches one of those (card counting) strategies is almost nil. It may match up after 20 hands, but after 100, there's no chance that it's just luck."

I think I'll order my martini now, shaken not stirred. But, seriously, let's look at this development from all angles.

First, I'm not sure how many casinos have actually bought and installed such a system (the article only mentioned one casino, Reno's El Dorado). Many such technological marvels have been announced never to be heard from again. So, we might want to wait and see whether this one catches on.

For one thing, the Nevada Gaming Commission is reportedly voicing objections to it. Casinos, under Nevada's gaming regulations, are apparently not supposed to use devices that *players* are similarly barred from using. It has specifically asked that casinos in Nevada not use these machines to count cards (which would seem to remove their primary purpose, although an El Dorado spokesman claims that the machines might also be used to parcel out player comps).

Second, MindPlay MP21s are not going to be able to detect players who use my playing and betting strategies, which are more advanced than the antiquated card counting methods it's been programmed to recognize. So, I, as a player, am not directly threatened by MindPlay's machines. Mr. Soltys has yet to catch up with my system.

But let's talk about the future health of the game. If this kind of thing became the norm, it would definitely create an adversarial attitude at the blackjack table. I'm not sure casinos would want that. I suspect that if MindPlay started to bounce players off the tables left and right, there might be a player backlash as well. The game would, at the very least, get a black eye, I imagine.

Are the computer nerds going to succeed some day, and take the fun out of the game? Let's be honest. We play blackjack because it's winnable and it's fun. Remove those two factors from the equation, and perhaps we'll all gather 'round the poker table!

Griffin GOLD
Makes Headlines:
A Blackjack Threat?

The December 21st, 2003 issue of the Los Angeles Times featured the article, "Card Counters Say Casinos Stack the Deck to Exclude Them." The villain in the article was Griffin GOLD and how casinos use the facial recognition software to bar anyone from blackjack cheats to card counters and "advantage players."

It opened up with the claim that one card counter who'd been on an MIT blackjack team had been confronted by "bad news guys" at an Atlantic City casino after having been "made" as a card counter, presumably by Griffin GOLD. That story surprised me. I started my career in Atlantic City and that was one place I remember as being the least likely to throw countermeasures at players. In fact, it is my understanding that New Jersey state law prevents casinos from barring players.

Nonetheless, the article goes on to quote a Las Vegas lawyer who's representing two alleged poker cheats: "In my opinion, [Griffin GOLD] is...peppered with mistakes and falsehoods based on some of the grossest hearsay." (Griffin

GOLD features a variety of mug shots of thousands of players they've identified as either cheats and thieves, or players who've been barred and/or suspected of using a system such as card counting.) If true, that suggests that government regulations might be necessary to control the proper use of eye-in-the-sky programs casinos are using.

In the L.A. Times article, Beverly Griffin, owner of Griffin Investigations (who sells the Griffin GOLD software), defended the use of Griffin GOLD in identifying card counters: "They took it from recreational to a business. They scout. They have people to count. They have people bring the money and place the bets. They are bankrolled." (Yet, that's not exactly correct. Very few counters are members of a team – organized or disorganized.)

The Times article makes this all sound sinister, and there might very well be a dark side to it. One guy in the article – the MIT card counting team member – claims Griffin might have been behind an alleged beating of one of the team's members (a claim Griffin steadfastly denies).

That claim aside (not having been proven), the thing that concerns me is the zeal in which casinos are going after smart players. Perhaps it is time to bring in the reigns a bit. Going after criminals and cheats is one thing; going after honest players in a similar fashion is over-zealous, at best. Plus, this kind of thing will hurt the game, in the long run.

In the meantime, players beware: in most areas, you can and will be barred if you're too good. So, get out the disguises, leave before they get too upset at how much you've won, and never give out your real name! (By the way, John Cleese of Monty Python fame hosted a fabulous TV show recently about *faces* in which he talked about facial recognition software. In fact, *he came up with a disguise that fooled the computers!* Wearing a broad-brimmed cap (like John Lennon used to wear) and large, dark-tinted glasses, his identity was not recognized. So it *can* be done!)

Blackjack Losers: Don't Make These Mistakes!

At a book event in Sante Fe, a woman told me about how her dad had incurred large losses playing blackjack.

"He ran up a big tab at the casino. Every time he played he'd lose, and then he'd bankroll his losses by increasing his tab. In the end, he owed the casino much more money than he had. He was in big trouble...our family was in big trouble...but, luckily, my father became the mayor of a town in California, and he traded political favors in lieu of paying the debt." She said the story was made into a book.

Her father was a loser. A *lucky* loser, but a *loser* nonetheless. Not in a pejorative way. But, in a financial sense.

I've heard variations on this story wherever I've gone. It's symptomatic of a very serious problem. And I've heard worse. I was told the story of a young father who shot himself to death after bankrupting the family through blackjack losses; that story particularly moved me to write this column. That's the kind of thing I want to try to prevent, through this little awareness campaign.

To that end, let's talk about *losers*, so that you never become one of them. These are the typical loser *types*:

1)*Wrong-school losers*: they made an honest effort to learn the game, but, sadly, they follow a betting system that is faulty.

2)*Delusionals*: these let infrequent wins delude them into thinking they're winners and have nothing more to learn; the truth is their losses are more frequent and larger than their wins.

3)*Get-rich quick losers*: they play blackjack like a roulette wheel, hoping to make a killing on one or two bets. They risk *all* their money, and often borrow from the casino after racking up huge losses. These are the suicides.

4)*Maximum bet losers*: Following irresponsible betting systems that recommend dramatic increases in betting according to the count, the lopsidedness of their betting approach quickly leaves them in the red.

5)*Martingale system desperados*: they keep raising their bet, hoping they'll eventually win, recoup their losses and make a few bucks. This is a quick way to mount big losses.

6)*Hot shot losers*: they crave attention, and make reckless large bets based not upon reason but upon a desire to be noticed. Their wins *will* be dramatic...but their losses even more so, and more frequent.

7)*Obsessive compulsives*: these folks have no control over themselves, but, sadly, are led astray by a mental illness that keeps them playing until there's nothing left.

8)*Marathoners*: they play for hours and hours, and usually at the same table. Some of them, in fact, are not to blame for their bad habits; they were taught (wrongly) that they should expect a steady stream of profits to come their way, every hour on the hour.

9)*Sad Sacks*: they are convinced the game is a matter of luck, or they don't have the capacity to learn the game, and so they go off half-cocked. They often ask fellow players what move to make, or, worse yet, the dealer. Many don't have much money to start with, and quickly get themselves in the hole.

10)*Beginners Luck types*: these players come in knowing very little about the game; they win a few hands through beginners luck, and go away thinking they're brilliant. The first time they play against cards that are not quite so good, they get bitter and leave the game for good, often winding up at the slot machines. One of these types surprised me when she admitted that she plays the slots "because I don't want to *think!*"

Hopefully, you did not recognize yourself when reading the above descriptions. If you did, you especially need to rethink your game!

Absolute Don'ts: Blackjack's Most Costly Mistakes

How many blackjack beginners have you seen, clutching an Old School Basic Strategy chart at the blackjack table, thinking that they held the secrets to winning in their hand?

It might be obvious to you, looking at these players, that they're in for a rude awakening. They don't realize how much goes into winning; nor do they know how wrong those charts often are.

But what you might not know is that many experienced players often make costly mistakes at the table, too.

Let's take a look at some of blackjack's absolute don'ts, to make sure you're not hurting your chances of coming out ahead.

Costly Mistake #1: Playing According To Basic Strategy

A new book on the market (that shall remain nameless) tells you that Basic Strategy is the best way to play for most players. He then goes on to say that it'll result in *losses* of 2% (he didn't quite put it that way; he said it would reduce the house edge to 2%). Given that reality, shouldn't he have warned players NOT to use basic strategy?

Coincidentally, I recently overheard a pit boss at a large Vegas Strip casino telling players the very same thing, at a blackjack lesson -- that the house had a 2% edge in blackjack. He offered no specifics on this pronouncement, by the way. A player's relative advantage or disadvantage versus the house actually varies, depending upon the game strategy he or she uses, the number of decks in place, the house rules...even the number of players at the table affects your likelihood of winning. (If you play according to MY Basic Strategy, you have anywhere from a 7% to a 14% advantage over the house depending on whether you're at a 6- or 7-player table, respectively, with a 1-deck game. Even so, I warn players in *Blackjack The SMART Way* that Basic Strategy is for beginners only. It just doesn't produce good enough results.)

The truth of the matter is that the inventors of the late-20th Century strategies *admitted* Basic Strategy's failings. Didn't *The World's Greatest Blackjack Book* (1980) say Basic Strategy players would "almost" break even – in other words, they'll *lose* (see page 193 of that book)? Didn't Edward Thorp tell readers in *Beat The Dealer* (1961) that Basic Strategy's benefits were *fractional?* (And that was based upon 1-deck games, dealt to the end!)

What's wrong with this picture? Imagine if you were assigned the task of designing a game strategy by your boss and you came up with a *losing* strategy; you'd probably be *fired*, wouldn't you?!

The point is, I don't have to prove that the Old School Basic Strategy approach is the *wrong* way to go (although I have many times over). The people who invented it *told* you how *poor* it was. Most players haven't gotten that message. Nor can they comprehend that someone would give them a game strategy that charts so poorly.

New Ways To Win MORE At Blackjack

Costly Mistake #2: Players Don't Know When To Leave

Many players seem to believe that blackjack tables are like fruit trees in season; the longer you sit there, the more fruit they'll reap. If they're losing, they tell themselves their "luck" will change soon, and the fruit of their efforts will begin to enrich their coffers soon.

Well blackjack is neither like a fruit tree (as some writers would lead you to believe), nor is it based upon luck. There are good mixes of cards, and bad (ask any poker player!).

You need to have *loss limits* on losing days AND, conversely, you need to know when to take your winnings and leave. If you consistently throw back your winnings because you play too long, or you lose more on losing days than you win on your average winning day, you will become a consistent loser. (You also need to learn how to identify whether the cards are good or bad!)

When I mention these general concepts at book events, most players say they *understand* them but they don't seem to be able to put them into *practice*.

That reminds me of the headline I saw in a radio studio while doing a guest appearance on a Las Vegas talk show. It said: "High Roller loses 52 Hands In A Row; Shoots Dealer."

Now, he might have been a high roller, but he wasn't a very astute player! (Nor is shooting the dealer ever a good strategy, I might add!)

More common are the players who take on losses that eclipse their gains.

A man from New Jersey once told me of a friend who had won $3,000 in Atlantic City.

"Great!" I said. "But, let me ask you a question: how much does he lose on losing days?"

"Oh migod," he said, "I've seen him lose $21,000."

Blackjack's Most Costly Mistakes

...So that player is wiping out more than SEVEN winning days' gains on losing days. That's the path to big losses.

Costly Mistake #3: Few Players Know How To Bet

Card strategy is just part of the picture. It's your *betting* strategy that really determines how much money you'll bring home. Yet, sadly, many a betting faux pas has led to disaster.

I've met too many people who have a story about someone who's committed *suicide* after one losing day! This particular phenomenon is often the result of high rollers hitting a wall with bad betting strategies. They played the game like it was roulette, banking on a big hit on one hand, playing with money they couldn't afford to lose, and then belatedly realized their mistake.

Blackjack is a game of attrition. Don't bank upon one round to make you rich. The way you make money off blackjack (and it's one of the most winnable games) is by winning more hands than you lose; and, by betting intelligently so that, when the cards are good, your bets are higher than when the cards are bad.

One of the WORST strategies is known as the Small-Martingale system, whereby players increase their bets to make up for losses in prior rounds. I saw this at a major Vegas casino recently.

A man placed a $200 bet and lost. The next round, he bet $300. Had he won, he'd have made up for the $200 loss, and come out $100 ahead; but he lost. He then placed a $1,000 bet (had he won, he would have made up for the $500 in losses, and come out $500 ahead – that was his thinking); but, he lost again.

The man let out air as though someone had kicked him in the stomach. The dealer, sensing this man's anguish, *stopped the game* to console the player! He'd lost what to him was a lot of money, *in three rounds*. He'd been raising his bets at the wrong time; the cards were bad! He'd mistakenly banked upon his *luck* changing.

This kind of betting strategy will get you into BIG trouble FAST. Plus, even if you have the dough to raise your bet dramatically each hand, table bet maximums make certain this chasing-losses approach will usually *fail...big time.*

Plus, there's no substitute for analyzing the cards and determining mathematically how to raise (and, perhaps LOWER) your bet.

In baseball, the season is not made or lost in a game; it's how many wins you have at the end. And that's how you should approach blackjack: with a conservative betting system that reaps the rewards of winning a maximum number of hands, and varying your bets conservatively and wisely.

Many more factors go into becoming a winner. But these are blackjack's biggest "DON'Ts."

On Tournaments, Countermeasures & Avoiding Getting Barred

Someone mailed me something recently that was published in a blackjack newsletter, and they wanted my reaction. It was this comment, from a letter to the editor:

"I am not a card counter, but casinos have discriminated against me simply because I participate in many blackjack tournaments so, therefore, they think I must be a card counter. Does this make any sense?"

The writer of that letter had fallen into a common trap that lures many unsuspecting players across the nation into trouble. **Indulging in casino blackjack tournaments goes against one of my fundamental principles - that *you must remain anonymous, or you're looking to attract casino scrutiny and countermeasures, and, possibly, even get barred.***

This player did not elaborate on what he meant by "discrimination," but he was clearly referring to something that was being done to hurt his ability to win. I take it he was being victimized by casino interference, or, as I more commonly refer to it, casino *countermeasures.*

Now, a casino's likelihood of resorting to countermeasures varies from casino to casino and from locale to locale. Some are quick to do so. Others are more player-friendly. (This, in fact, is one of the things you should take into account in picking a good casino at which to play.)

And, unfortunately, as the player who wrote the letter I quoted at the beginning found out, in signing up for tournaments, there's sometimes a price to pay. All the skills in the world won't help you much if you open yourself up to unwanted, negative interference.

Now, understand that all good blackjack authors, whether they were professional players or just occasional hobbyists, have reported experiencing this – from Thorp, to Revere, Uston, Humble/Cooper, on up to present day player/authors such as myself. **The possibility of casino interference is an everyday fact of life for the blackjack player.**

The Need For Awareness

I want you to take away from this column a whole new awareness. *You need to pay attention to what's going on around you. And you must react to any harmful interference you've detected.*

For instance, at a large Las Vegas Strip casino recently, I was doing extremely well. I had lost just one round in 30-40 minutes! Then, something interesting happened.

The dealer dropped a card on the floor. To the untrained eye, it might have appeared like a clumsy mistake.

But this dealer was a real pro; her dropping of the card had been *intentional.* She made a big deal about it, in fact, if you had eyes to see. She ever-so-slowly bent over to retrieve it.

By the time she'd stood back up, a new dealer AND the pit boss AND two new decks of cards had arrived at the table.

What would you have done in this situation? (Hint: none of

my fellow players did a thing. They either didn't notice what was going on, or they didn't understand its dire significance.)

I immediately got up and left. Why?

The dealer's signal (the dropping of the card) meant: *someone's winning too much here...replace the cards and bring in a new dealer...let's do something to win this money back.*

That told me that: 1) *the casino was upset at how much I'd won;* 2) *they were now going to watch me closely;* and, 3) *they were using countermeasures, such as removing the cards that had been so good for me, to try to take my winnings back.*

Such a counterreaction indicated the casino was uncomfortable with my winning rate and was annoyed with me. This was nothing to ignore.

A Casino's Comfort Zone

Understand: every casino has its *comfort zone* regarding player gains. Some casinos don't seem to mind your winning thousands of dollars; others seem jealous of every chip you win. Part of your job is to figure out what each casino's comfort zone is, and then *stay within it.*

That means that once you've won an amount that's likely to provoke unwanted scrutiny and countermeasures, you should get ready to *leave* on the first sign that casino personnel are getting aggravated with you. You don't want to stick around when you know the casino has begun an active campaign to hurt your game. *You cannot win in the face of that.*

Keep your eyes open. Upon any sign of being "watched" (if a pit boss, for example, is giving you the evil eye), it's time to leave. (In the case of a pit boss breathing down my neck, however, I sometimes try this ruse: I'll make a *terrible* move! Often, upon seeing that, the pit boss leaves the table and mutters something about how horrible I am as a player and the battle is won: the heat is off.)

Upon noticing any countermeasures, it's time to leave. For instance, *it's always a good idea to leave when new cards are brought in, especially after you've accumulated a good amount of chips.* There are such things as good cards and bad cards. My computer research has proven that, once cards that were real good for you are replaced, it's statistically unlikely that you'll do as well with the new decks as you did with the old. Why throw back your winnings?

Other countermeasures to be aware of:

If you're winning a lot and a new dealer's brought in at an odd time (outside the normal shift change time), it's always time to cash in your chips. This often signals rough times ahead –this dealer might very well be "luckier" than the last one.

If the dealer begins to shuffle up on you after giving you just one round of cards, it's time to leave. Such a change indicates the casino is trying to make you lose; in doing this, they remove the profitable predicability factor that exists when you are dealt more rounds.

At the most extreme end of the interference spectrum is the risk of getting barred. No matter how advanced your skills, you cannot profit from those skills if you cannot play.

Although Atlantic City casinos are forbidden by state law to selectively exclude players simply because they're winners, you should always keep in mind that most other casinos can bar you from playing if they wish, for any reason. It's a regrettable reality of which blackjack players absolutely have to be aware.

Why should you care? Here are two cautionary tales that demonstrate why this issue speaks directly to you:

A young man once approached me at one of my New Mexico book signing events and told me he'd been barred from a local casino. He pulled me aside, to ask me what he'd done wrong, and how he could avoid this from happening in the future. (His mother had been on one of the legendary Ken Uston blackjack teams, so this guy was no dope.)

Upon asking him a few questions, here's the story that emerged: He was playing at a casino that was holding a drawing for a prize, and he was specifically approached by a pit boss, and urged to fill one out. Within minutes, the boss returned and announced: "Congratulations, Mr. X! You've just been BARRED from playing at this casino!"

Ouch! That took a bite out of his blackjack income potential.

But he could have avoided all of that had he read up on my playing approach beforehand, which includes all the many NON-card-strategy issues that go into becoming a consistent winner. He broke one of my cardinal rules: *stay anonymous at all costs.*

Then there was this cautionary tale:

A player I met at an Arizona book signing event who told me he'd been playing at a casino in Japan when a player sat to his right and played one hand. The pit boss then rushed over and told the new player to leave the casino.

"Why?" the man asked.

"Because you were barred in Laughlin (Nevada)," came the response.

The casino in Japan obviously was using facial-recognition software connected to the "eye in the sky" cameras that focus on each table (which is not uncommon). They also undoubtedly had this connected to databases of the faces of players who were barred from other casinos around the world.

The first story demonstrates why *you should never give your real name, address or phone number to any casino.* The second story shows you that *there are often consequences if you blow your anonymity, including possibly the inability to play blackjack not just at the casino that bars you, but also at many casinos throughout the world whose databases are connected to that casino's database.* This is just one way in which today's technology has changed the world of blackjack.

Now, you may think, "Gee, I'm only a beginner, so I don't have to worry about all of this!" But, if you don't worry about it as a beginner, you're likely to find out later why that was a foolish policy.

If you blow your anonymity at any point – you've joined up for blackjack tournaments, filled out contest forms, signed up for comp cards, or accepted travel junkets – you cannot later erase your known identity when and if a casino decides to bar you once you've become a good player.

Now, some notable players have boasted about how many casinos have barred them. But I don't think that's a badge of honor. I prefer to AVOID that eventuality so that I can keep playing (and winning), and so I behave accordingly.

Another thought along these lines:

If a casino boss asks you your name, *leave* (make a joke, small talk, whatever, and then graciously walk away). If you don't, you might win the battle (that is, you'll maximize your gains for that day) and lose the war (a boss asking for your name indicates you're likely to get barred).

And here's one last idea -- a creative way of responding to the threat of being barred:

If you're a consistent winner and you've often gotten heat for it, you might consider buying a book about how to put on disguises. Going this route is actually a lot of fun, and it'll prolong your playing days. A lot of us, in fact, have availed ourselves of that option.*

---

* For more comprehensive information on casino countermeasures see Chapter 11 of *Blackjack The SMART Way.*

The
Mahowney
Treatment

If you saw the movie Owning Mahowney and you weren't shaken up on some level by the degree of scrutiny players get by casino personnel – from the eye-in-the-sky surveillance monitoring crew on up to the top bosses – then you weren't putting yourself in Mahowney's shoes.

Mind you, Mahowney, a character based on fact, was admittedly a sad sack with a compulsive gambling problem that drove him to steal more than $10 million dollars from the Canadian bank at which he worked. You and I are not in his category.

But it wasn't his nefarious dealings that led to his getting an inordinate amount of scrutiny. It was simply the fact that he flashed a lot of cash around and made larger bets than just about anyone else at the time. (He blew millions of dollars in an evening, and this was in the early 1980s.)

The scary thing about it – if the movie portrays this story with any accuracy – is that Mahowney's *every* move was being watched, 24/7. When he went to Vegas, a casino boss *in another town* (who had benefited from Mahowney's reckless gambling style before) *knew about it instantly* and even commanded his men to *fly out there to do something to bring him back to their casino* before Mahowney lost the winnings he'd made that night (which they apparently *knew to the penny*). This same casino boss even reportedly hired a private investigator do an extensive and intrusive profile on Mahowney. Not one crime was committed in this regard, but it was kind of *creepy.*

It's a movie every player must see. It's an object lesson in what you should NOT to do.

Who wants to get *the Mahowney treatment?*

I've said this for years: never be the high roller at the table, because it draws too much attention. If you take a high rollers' private table for yourself, understand that you're attracting a LOT of unwanted scrutiny.

Granted, all of us will be watched by the eye-in-the-sky guys, and that's not a crime. But we want to blend into the crowd, remain anonymous.

Mahowney was flattered by the casino fawning his lavish displays of stupid betting inspired. He took it as an honor that he was given free luxurious suites and other favors. But, behind the scenes, the bosses at his favorite casino were – according to the movie – attempting to manipulate him into losing all of his money (even prohibiting his girlfriend from interrupting him at a craps table).

A player once told me another cautionary tale regarding accepting casino favors. He, too, liked to throw a lot of money around. As a result, he was given a free stay in an impressive suite at a prestigious casino. He felt like a big shot.

Before leaving, though, he was approached by several casino personnel who told him in no uncertain terms that he would never again be welcome at that establishment.

The Mahowney Treatment

"Why?" he asked, stunned.

"Because you only played here for two hours, the whole weekend!" was the reply.

They'd been watching him, 24/7. How else would they have known exactly how little he'd played there?

Remember the Milton Friedman adage: "There's no such thing as a free lunch."

Casino favors, however nice they may seem, come with strings attached.

If you're smart, you'll want to avoid *the Mahowney treatment*. So: keep to yourself; dress in a modest fashion; keep chatter to a minimum (revealing nothing personal, including your name); make modest bets; and avoid being showy. There's a down side to being a big shot.

Anonymity is a prize to be protected.

Report From Vegas: The Casino Blackjack Lesson

It has always been my contention that casino blackjack lessons are misleading at best. It's a good way to go wrong.

A case in point: a blackjack lesson I witnessed recently at a major Vegas casino. It started 20 minutes late, causing several attendees to leave beforehand, yet the teacher (the dealer) was there all the time, lazily shuffling the cards!

At 12:20, he suddenly asked: "How many of you have never played blackjack?" Most raised their hands. "OK," he said, dealing everyone cards without explaining the game.

With an up card of 9, he said: "With a 9, always assume the dealer has a 19!" That's hogwash! Ten-pointers make up just 31% of the deck. With this dealer's strategy, you'll be correct 31% of the time and wrong *69% of the time!*

He then mumbled recommendations to each player. The general rule, he announced, was to draw to a 17. He made it sound as if that's all they needed to know. Then, a player with a soft 18 (an Ace and a 7) was told to STAND! He offered no advice on betting, except that, "The way players make a lot of money is by increasing their bet with each hand." This horrible advice caused one player to run out of chips in 10 minutes; the rest were nearly out in 15 minutes!

The second round the up card was a 10. He told a player with 10 points: "You only double on 10s versus the dealer's low cards." Wrong! He gave no other information on doubling, and the only advice he gave on splitting was: "*Always* split your Aces!" Wrong! Books going back to *1961* have noted there are times when you should *not* to split Aces. Later that round, he made no comment when a player *stood* on a 16 when her best move was to surrender (an option offered there)! In fact, he later misled them by saying: "Surrender is never smart; you lose half your bet."

The next round, with an Ace up, he said "never take Insurance – it's always bad." Wrong again! Plus, I wondered why he suddenly changed his tune. Hadn't he told the players to *always assume the dealer has a 10 in the hole?*

The following round, with a 3 showing, the dealer told a player "always *stand* with a 12 versus the dealer's 3," which is wacko! The pit boss then came over and tried to reinforce this mistaken logic, removing the hole card and replacing it with a 10! "Let the dealer bust!" he said. His ruse backfired, however, when the dealer drew an 8, giving him a 21. "That's life!" he said, brushing off his mistake. The pit boss then told the players to buy a Basic Strategy chart from the gift shop and ALWAYS play by its rules: "if you don't play Basic Strategy, the house has a 9% edge; if you play Basic, the house has a 2% edge, so you're almost even." This was one of the few semi-true things said during that lesson. He *admitted* that Basic Strategy is a *losing* strategy! Yet, no one asked why he urged them to follow it!

In another round, with a 4, the dealer told everyone with stiffs to *stand* (which is OK)...and *that* was the *whole* lesson! It's a shame this casino is misleading players. But, until things change, beware of free casino blackjack lessons!

They're Rare
But They're There:
Cheating Dealers -- Part One

The female blackjack dealer appeared a bit clumsy. That's all I had noticed; it made me a bit uneasy. Suddenly, the pit boss came over to berate her.

"No, no, no!" he snapped, rearranging the chips she had stacked in coloring in a player. "You should stack them in groups of five, not six!"

She was about to give the player $125 in exchange for his $150 in chips. By stacking his chips in groups of six, it appeared as if he'd had $25 less than he in fact possessed.

The first baseman left immediately. By the disdain on his face, he obviously thought the dealer had shorted the player intentionally.

I stayed around for another round, partly out of curiosity.

I drew a pair of 8s, which I split. One of my new hands drew to a 19; with the other, I had received a 3, and, upon doubling, I drew a 10, for 21 points. The dealer pulled a 21.

Cheating Dealers -- Part One

The dealer then collected ALL of my chips!

"Wait a minute," I said. "I pushed on this hand."

Without a blink, she gave me two $25 chips.

"Wait a minute!" I shouted. "I doubled on that one, too!"

Without a comment, she swiftly gave me two more green chips.

If she hadn't intentionally meant to cheat me (once by taking *all* of my chips, and again by giving me *half* of what she owed me) why did she take my word for it without a pause or an argument? I have no doubt she intended to pocket my chips. After seeing her operate for only two rounds, I didn't stick around for more.

At another casino, I was flipping a $25 chip with one hand while the dealer collected the cards from the last round when a loud sound to my right made me turn around and drop the chip. Turning back around, I saw the dealer slip some cards under my chip, flip it into his free hand and pocket it!

I nearly slugged him, but I caught myself. Had I argued over the theft, the ensuing argument would have drawn way too much unwanted attention. They would never have forgotten my face after that brouhaha. Remember – we avoid being barred by remaining anonymous.

Instead, I left, whispering to another player, "Watch your chips. The dealer just took one of mine."

That was definitely a rogue dealer, acting on his own. No casino, not even one that was thoroughly crooked, would sanction such a brazen move.

I made a note of the guy's name and his appearance. I'd never sit at his table ever again.

At a small casino on Las Vegas' Strip, I sat down to play double deck action when, in losing several hands in a row, I noticed something curious. The mix of the cards seemed pre-planned, in a disastrous fashion. They were coming out high-low-high-low, etc. That kind of mix produces a lot of busting hands.

Then, when it came time to shuffle, the dealer did something strange. He put the cards on the table and chatted up the players. Then...*he started dealing again without having shuffled the cards!!!*

That was clearly intentional. I glared at him, letting him know I caught what he had done. He sneered right back at me, letting me know he didn't care I'd caught him cheating.

Was he doing this at the behest of the casino, to keep the bad cards going and rip the players off? Maybe, maybe not. But I didn't stick around to find out.

Bad dealers are rare, but they're there. More next time.

They're Rare
But They're There:
Cheating Dealers -- Part Two

At a casino in Nevada, I suspected the dealer was dealing seconds – in other words, occasionally dealing cards other than the top card, to make players bust and make his hands NOT.

Two big-bet hot shots were to my right. One of them made a fatal mistake.

"Give me a 10!" he told the dealer. (Never tell the dealer what you want! They might not be on your side!)

"I can do better than that!" the dealer boasted. "What SUIT would you like?"

With that, he dealt the player a 10 – *by sliding the top card to the side with his left thumb and dealing the second card with his right thumb.*

I got up from the table without comment and watched a few more rounds.

New Ways To Win MORE At Blackjack

The hot shots – believing the dealer was helping them win (which is exactly what the dealer wanted them to think) – dramatically raised their bets. To their surprise, the dealer then wiped them out of *thousands* of dollars in three successive losing rounds...

At a casino elsewhere, I chose a table where the dealer had been chatting with another player for a long period of time *without dealing the cards* (that, I realized later, was a warning signal). I was the only other player at the table (another mistake; in research I conducted later, I discovered that you *cannot* win, in the long term, at 2-player tables).

The dealer then dealt the cards — *without shuffling* – and a pattern developed I'd never encountered before. The cards came out, round after round, in a very pat ascending-totals sequential order. I'd get 19 points, the guy to my left, 20, and the dealer would get 21.

After losing five rounds in a row in this suspicious fashion, I got up and left. I was certain the cards had been rigged in advance.

I later learned that what I had run into was a *cooler deck* – a pre-arranged set of cards designed to make all players lose every round...

At another casino, I witnessed the dealer brazenly *rearranging* the cards *after* the round, into a killer high-low-high-low sequence...

At a book event once, I met a dealer who claimed he knew of a casino that was *removing some Aces and 9s* from pitch game decks, to hurt players' chances of winning...

On a cable TV documentary, a dealer was shown, on videotape, *making a blackjack for himself!* (The casino, in providing the tape, clearly did not approve of his dishonesty.) The dealer's up card was an Ace. Peeking at his hole card, he saw it was a 6; in a sleight of hand trick with his left hand, he replaced it with a 10, wiping out all the play-

Cheating Dealers -- Part Two

ers...

Every casino has a security staff whose job is to ferret out (and fire) dealers who cheat. You might, however, be unlucky enough to find yourself, on a rare occasion, facing one of these jerks. You don't have to become their next victim, however.

(I'm not the first one to write about this, by the way. Thorp, Revere, Wong, Humble/Cooper and others have too. I'm only reporting what I have seen. Human nature being what it is, whenever money's involved it's a good idea to keep on your toes.)

Be Proactive

What can you do to avoid being cheated? Here is my advice:

Number one, try to play at tables where the dealer deals *slowly* and shows you the *top* of the deck, so you can see the tops of the cards as he or she deals (they're less likely to be dealing seconds). Number two, play at casinos that are overseen by a state gaming commission. Number three, don't get paranoid, but leave a table: a) after losing five hands in a row; b) if the dealer flips a card onto the table with the hand holding the cards; and c) if the cards come out in a recognizable, killer pre-set sequence.*

Cheaters are rare, but they're there.

* For more details, see Chapter 11 of *Blackjack The SMART Way*.

Increase Your Winning Potential: Keep A Blackjack Notebook

Do you keep a blackjack notebook? (I used to urge players to keep a blackjack "diary," but I think the word diary has negative connotations, to men especially.)

You probably don't realize how important a tool a notebook is, in helping to increase your winning rates. It may take a little time and effort, but, really, not much, and it's well worth the investment. (This is another example, by the way, of how many factors go into becoming a big winner at blackjack.)

There are many ways of going about this. You can use notebook-type hole-punched graph paper and make a grid like I'm going to show you, writing in your notebook with a pen or pencil...or (better yet), you can use a spreadsheet program on your computer.

Divide your graph paper or spreadsheet into columns with these headers: Day/ Date/Time; Casino; Dealers; Casino Bosses; Game(s); Bet Minimum; Won/Lost (or W/L); Win Ratio; Tips; Notes; and Your Appearance.

Increase Your Winning Potential: Keep A Notebook

Under "Day/Day/Time," be sure to include the specific duration of your playing session (for example: "1:15-2:30 p.m."). This tells you not only how long you played, but the casino shift during which you played. You might find, for instance, that losses come on days you played too long. You might find that you do better on some days versus others. (Are weeknights better than weekends? Are holidays good times or bad times to play? This is what you'll find out.) You need to know what *time* you played if you decide that the casino boss on that shift was giving you too much flak, and you need to avoid playing during his or her shift next time.

Under "Casino," identify the names and the locations (some casinos have offshoots by the same name). This is important, for one thing, because you do not want to wear out your welcome at any one casino. If you see you've been going back to one casino too often (if winning there), give it a rest. Note whether the casinos were good or bad, too. In avoiding the bad ones, you'll spare yourself certain losses.

Under "Dealers," write their names and descriptions, and, where appropriate, a brief comment, if there's something negative or positive to record. This might be, "Seek out next time; gave 95% penetration with heavy toking." Or, simply, "Avoid!" Descriptions are imperative because this will enable you to smoothly seek out or avoid tables of the dealers with whom you've had experience, without making it obvious by straining to read their name tags. Foreknowledge of dealers is extremely powerful in increasing your winning potential. (Do the same in the "Bosses" column.)

In the "Games" column, record the number of decks and any negative restrictions or positive offerings (such as surrender). This will give you an idea of what game you win at the most (and, therefore, you should concentrate on). Plus, it will remind you of casinos with rules that enable you to win more, so that you especially patronize those.

Under "Bet Minimum" write not only what the table minimum was, but, if different, what minimum bet you chose

to make (it might have been above the table minimum) --
this will tell you what minimum produces the best results for
you -- within your comfort zone.

In the "Won/Lost" column, record the money you won or
lost that session. The "Win Ratio" column, in contrast, is to
keep a running tab on the number of winning sessions
you've had overall. You should have a fraction -- the top
number being your number of winning sessions, divided by
your total number of sessions -- equalling a percentage,
which is your winning percentage. This tells you how successful you are, and whether you need to do something to
improve your skills (or not). Preferably, you'd like to see this
grow to where it's in the 80-percentile range.

"Tips" are listed because they might be tax deductible
(consult your tax advisor). If they're not, leave this out.

The "Notes" column is for anything significant in the way
of experiences or observations. What was the penetration?
Do you want to go back? Get any heat from casino bosses?

Under "Your Appearance," record exactly how you looked
(from your clothes, to your headgear, eyewear and hair-
style). This is crucial if you ran into countermeasures or if
you won a lot of money; you'll want to radically alter how
you dress the next time to reduce the potential for trouble
(getting barred, or being subjected to interference).

By the way -- I suggest that you keep two blackjack note-
books: one for when you're first investigating a new town
or casino; another for towns and casinos with which you're
already familiar. Your winning rate will be lower (and less
accurate) during what I call your *exploratory phase* in a new
town or casino (you haven't yet weeded out the bad casinos
and dealers from your playing schedule).

Give this a try. You'll be a surprised at how much a blackjack notebook can add to your bottom line.

Sample Blackjack Notebook & Entry

Day/Date/Time	Casino	Dealers	Bosses	Games	Bet Min.	W/L	Win Ratio	Tips	Notes	Your Appearance
Sunday 2/28/2004 2-3:10 p.m.	The Any Casino Anytown, NV	Fred (Mohawk haircut in his 40s) Gives you two rounds w/7-players if you tip him well. Nancy (Short blonde w/horn-rimmed glasses) To be avoided. Surly, deals way too fast and makes mistakes.	Pete (Looks like Swartzenegger) Brought in new dealer after I'd won $1700. (Countermeasure.) Asked me my name just before I left -- try to avoid his shift in the future.	1-deck Allows surrender.	$50	$1,565 (after tips)	888/1000=88.80%	$100	Seems like their "comfort zone" is below $1500 in winnings.	Tux, glasses, goatee, Rolex watch, long hair, long bushy sideburns.

A Common Player Attitude Problem

There's an attitude I hear expressed by a lot of blackjack players...it goes something like this: "I'm taking 'x' amount of dollars, and when I lose that, I'm done!" This is usually said cheerfully, with a *smile!*

Imagine a professional baseball pitcher going into a game with that attitude. He'd say: "I'm going out there, and when the other team's hit five homeruns, I'm outta there!" Now imagine him *smiling* while saying that!!

What's wrong with this picture?

The first thing that's wrong is that this mindset predestines the player to lose. It's a self-fulfilling prophecy. It also lulls players' brains to sleep - *they won't get up from a table until they have, indeed, lost the amount they set out to lose.*

Sometimes, too, the amount they say they'll accept in losses is ridiculously small — $50 to $100. They don't take bad tables or bad betting spots into account, for instance. Just because you've experienced one bad table or betting

A Common Player Attitude Problem

spot doesn't mean it's time to give up the game!

Beyond that — no matter what the pursuit — a basic requirement for winning is that you need to have a winner's *attitude*. If you've ever played organized sports, you know that the better athletes have elevated this to a science. Coaches spend an inordinate amount of pre-game time "psyching" the team into visualizing a positive outcome, so that they go into the game *expecting* to win. They know this is the key to winning consistently.

In a similar way, you have to psyche yourself into winning before you enter the casino's doors. BUT, there's more to it than that.

Sports teams ALSO ensure success by reviewing play strategy before they hit the field. This is also important to a blackjack player's achieving a high winning rate.

There are so many factors that go into winning at blackjack – especially given the many new method innovations and card behavior discoveries produced by my research. Even I sit down for a half hour to an hour before playing to review my plan for the day, making sure I don't forget anything – even though I *created* the system I'm using! (Think of it: even Beethoven himself had to practice his own piano concertos before he went onstage.)

Too many blackjack players go up to the table cold and then wonder why they came away losers. A major actress the other day said she'd been taught to come to the movie set *in character*, and then to *stay* in character throughout the working day, *because it was much easier than revving up her imagination for each scene, from a cold state.* This same principle applies to the blackjack player. It's hard to rev up all the thinking gears in a split second upon arriving at the table — especially given the casino distractions (the noise, the lights, etc.). So, after practicing and/or reviewing your notes at home or at the hotel, you then need to *think* blackjack every second of the way on your journey to the casino and then to the table.

Another thing wrong with the attitude expressed up top is that it presumes that blackjack is an exercise in futility, and therefore it's unnecessary to take the time to develop playing skills. In other words: if winning is impossible, why bother to study the game?

I counter that question with one of my own: if that's a player's (mistaken) attitude, why does he or she bother playing at all?

You're not really playing blackjack unless: 1) you've studied a good system; 2) you've practiced at home for many weeks until you're winning more than not; and, 3) you've arrived at a mental state where you're *expecting* to win.

More on *how* to practice in my next column.

To Win Big
You Need To
Practice Correctly

Many have asked me to recommend what *software* they should use in practicing the methods they learned in *Cutting Edge Blackjack* and *Blackjack The SMART Way*. A Colorado Gambler reader felt the *speed* he could gain with a computerized game made it better than the use of real cards.

Practicing is crucial to your becoming a great player. Yet, because many of the players who indeed practice are going about it wrongly, I think we need to review how to do this.

"Speed" and "practicing" are two words that should never be used in the same sentence. Speed only hurts your ability to benefit from practice sessions. Those of you who have you taken lessons on a musical instrument know what I'm talking about. No smart music teacher encourages you rip through a piece of music in order to play it better. He or she always takes a slower-than-normal approach with beginners.

The same approach should be taken with blackjack. You need to take your sweet time when practicing methods that are new to you. It is not speed that enlightens. It's the level of brain activity you exert. In other words – you need to engage your brain and really study what's happening in each round, in order to develop a quicker response time and a skill level that brings you maximum gains. Music teachers will tell you: practise slowly; speed will come with time. As with music, you should be more concerned about how *well* you're using what you learned rather than how *quickly* you make a move. Speed is not what makes you a winner. Yet that's strike one against computerized blackjack games: they make players speed through practice sessions.

Blackjack software is admittedly *seductive* and visually *exciting*. But don't let this override your understanding that these games are not the practice tools you need. Don't be a slave to the software; practice properly, with cards.

True, too -- software-simulated blackjack requires less *effort* than the use of real cards, which adds to its attraction. But in this attraction lies another problem. There is an *addictive* quality to computerized games, psychologically, which is bad in and of itself. This lulls a player's brain to sleep. Studies have proven that TV viewing turns off your brain's alpha waves (which conduct thinking processes), causing *beta waves* to take over (which induce a passive, trancelike state). The same is true of computer screens.

Another thing. Unless you plan on playing Internet blackjack or Digital 21 at the casino (options I don't recommend, for their lower winning potential and randomness), computer-simulated blackjack games will not accurately reflect the realities you will experience at the casino. So, using them to practice will *hurt* your ability to improve.

Cards don't play out randomly. For instance, in the computer studies of card behavior that led to *Cutting Edge Blackjack*, I discovered there are many *repeating phenomena* going on from shuffle to shuffle due to standardized casino shuffling. These phenomena will not be reproduced in a software-simulated game. Computerized games use a computer's *random* number generator to "deal" the cards. Unlike the real game, the "cards" are "dealt" randomly. To

To Win Big You Need To Practice Correctly

profit from repeating phenomena, you must know how to *detect* them. But, how can you develop these skills when these games have no repeating patterns to detect?

Plus, using real cards in practicing forces you to learn the ins and outs of casino shuffling and the formalized collection of spent hands. This admittedly requires more effort on your part -- you must study the exacting, standardized way in which your favorite casinos shuffle the cards and then collect them; then, you must reproduce that activity in the playing out of practice rounds. But your effort will be amply rewarded. *Reproducing casino card handling at home will teach you how the shuffling methods at your favorite casinos reorder the cards. You will then be able to tap into the very valuable skill of shuffle tracking* (which I introduced to you in a prior column). Similarly, by using real cards, you'll be able to practice cutting the cards, to develop a dead-on eye for following them through the shuffle. (Before dealing the cards, you should look and see if you indeed placed the cut card properly, to bring back the cards you wanted to.) By playing everything out slowly, you can also observe how *the collection of cards sometimes results in fortuitous card groupings in the discard pile* (which you'd then want to follow through the next shuffle).

By using cards, you can also (by documenting the exact order of the cards following each shuffle) replay rounds *differently.* Keeping the order of the cards exactly the same as they were following the last shuffle, but having certain players make *different* card choices, you can then fully comprehend why *you need to tailor-make your card strategy to adjust to the mix of cards that have been dealt ahead of your turn.* Depending on that mix, your plan of action will differ (because the probability of getting any hit cards you might need will change as the mix of *undealt* cards changes). I don't know of any software that would allow you to replay rounds in this way.

I think you'll get to like practicing with cards. Especially when you see how much it improves your game.

178

Index

Index

Index

About The Author

One of the few bestselling blackjack authors who's both an expert player and a computer researcher who's developed many innovations and advancements in player strategies, Richard Harvey's blackjack career began in Atlantic City after being a victim of corporate layoffs. The system he used, which he'd developed in the two years beforehand, sprang from a love of cards (he was a New York City Bridge club player) and math (he'd minored in theoretical math and statistics in college; he later also studied computer science, in post-graduate school).

His decision to create his own blackjack system was born out of frustration at his lack of success testing others' methods in computer trials. His approach has been greatly refined over the years, but even his early experiences at the blackjack table were highly profitable. Mr. Harvey's latest monumental computer research project resulted in many incredible and historic breakthroughs. The end result was his creation of the first entirely new and better way of playing the game in more than 40 years.

Since 1999, Mr. Harvey has been on 100+ talk shows in the USA and elsewhere, and he's has been written up in countless favorable newspaper and magazine write-ups. He continues to do blackjack research, play blackjack, write syndicated columns, give seminars and write books. He says he is especially proud of the fact that so many readers have gone on to great success using his unique approach to the game.

Take A Seminar!

Mystic Ridge Books is a proud sponsor of Richard Harvey's highly-acclaimed seminars, held from coast-to-coast. Many players have flown *hundreds of miles* to attend one!

Get on our mailing list so we can let you know when these events are scheduled! Send your name, address and phone number to: Mystic Ridge Books, P.O. Box 66930, Albuquerque, NM 87193. Or register for a future seminar through our web site www.blackjacktoday.com.